Battleground
NORM...

JUNO BEACH
3RD CANADIAN & 79TH ARMOURED DIVISIONS

Other guides in the Battleground Europe Series:

Walking the Salient by Paul Reed
Ypres - Sanctuary Wood and Hooge by Nigel Cave
Ypres - Hill 60 by Nigel Cave
Ypres - Messines Ridge by Peter Oldham
Ypres - Polygon Wood by Nigel Cave
Ypres - Passchendaele by Nigel Cave
Ypres - Airfields and Airmen by Michael O'Connor
Ypres - St Julien by Graham Keech

Walking the Somme by Paul Reed
Somme - Gommecourt by Nigel Cave
Somme - Serre by Jack Horsfall & Nigel Cave
Somme - Beaumont Hamel by Nigel Cave
Somme - Thiepval by Michael Stedman
Somme - La Boiselle by Michael Stedman
Somme - Fricourt by Michael Stedman
Somme - Carnoy-Montauban by Graham Maddocks
Somme - Pozieres by Graham Keech
Somme - Courcelette by Paul Reed
Somme - Boom Ravine by Trevor Pidgeon
Somme - Mametz Wood by Michael Renshaw
Somme - Delville Wood by Nigel Cave
Somme - Advance to Victory (North) 1918 by Michael Stedman
Somme - Flers by Trevor Pidgeon
Somme - Bazentin Ridge by Edward Hancock
Somme - Combles by Paul Reed
Somme - Beaucourt by Michael Renshaw
Somme - Hamel by Peter Pedersen
Somme - Airfields and Airmen by Michael O'Connor

Arras - Vimy Ridge by Nigel Cave
Arras - Gavrelle by Trevor Tasker and Kyle Tallett
Arras - Bullecourt by Graham Keech
Arras - Monchy le Preux by Colin Fox

Hindenburg Line by Peter Oldham
Hindenburg Line Epehy by Bill Mitchinson
Hindenburg Line Riqueval by Bill Mitchinson
Hindenburg Line Villers-Plouich by Bill Mitchinson
Hindenburg Line - Cambrai by Jack Horsfall & Nigel Cave
Hindenburg Line - Saint Quentin by Helen McPhail and Philip Guest
Hindenburg Line -Bourlon Wood by Jack Horsfall & Nigel Cave
Cambrai - Airfields and Airmen by Michael O'Connor

La Bassée - Neuve Chapelle by Geoffrey Bridger
Loos - Hohenzollen Redoubt by Andrew Rawson
Loos - Hill 70 by Andrew Rawson
Fromelles by Peter Pedersen

Mons by Jack Horsfall and Nigel Cave

Accrington Pals Trail by William Turner

Poets at War: Wilfred Owen by Helen McPhail and Philip Guest

Poets at War: Edmund Blunden by Helen McPhail and Philip Gu...
Poets at War: Graves & Sassoon by Helen McPhail and Philip G...
Gallipoli by Nigel Steel
Gallipoli - Gully Ravine by Stephen Chambers
Gallipoli - Landings at Helles by Huw & Jill Rodge
Walking the Italian Front by Francis Mackay
Italy - Asiago by Francis Mackay

Verdun: Fort Doumont by Christina Holstein

Boer War - The Relief of Ladysmith by Lewis Childs
Boer War - The Siege of Ladysmith by Lewis Childs
Boer War - Kimberley by Lewis Childs
Isandlwana by Ian Knight and Ian Castle
Rorkes Drift by Ian Knight and Ian Castle

Stamford Bridge & Hastings by Peter Marren
Wars of the Roses - Wakefield/ Towton by Philip A. Haigh
English Civil War - Naseby by Martin Marix Evans, Peter Burton
Michael Westaway
English Civil War - Marston Moor by David Clark
War of the Spanish Succession - Blenheim 1704 by James Falk...
Napoleonic - Hougoumont by Julian Paget and Derek Saunder...
Napoleonic - Waterloo by Andrew Uffindell and Michael Coru...

WW2 Dunkirk by Patrick Wilson
WW2 Calais by Jon Cooksey
WW2 Boulogne by Jon Cooksey
WW2 Normandy - Pegasus Bridge/Merville Battery by Carl Shil...
WW2 Normandy - Utah Beach by Carl Shilleto
WW2 Normandy - Omaha Beach by Tim Kilvert-Jones
WW2 Normandy - Gold Beach by Christopher Dunphie & Garry Joh...
WW2 Normandy - Gold Beach Jig by Tim Saunders
WW2 Normandy - Juno Beach by Tim Saunders
WW2 Normandy - Sword Beach by Tim Kilvert-Jones
WW2 Normandy - Operation Bluecoat by Ian Daglish
WW2 Normandy - Operation Goodwood by Ian Daglish
WW2 Normandy - Epsom by Tim Saunders
WW2 Normandy - Hill 112 by Tim Saunders
WW2 Normandy - Mont Pinçon by Eric Hunt
WW2 Normandy - Cherbourg by Andrew Rawson
WW2 Das Reich – Drive to Normandy by Philip Vickers
WW2 Oradour by Philip Beck
WW2 Market Garden - Nijmegen by Tim Saunders
WW2 Market Garden - Hell's Highway by Tim Saunders
WW2 Market Garden - Arnhem, Oosterbeek by Frank Steer
WW2 Market Garden - Arnhem, The Bridge by Frank Steer
WW2 Market Garden - The Island by Tim Saunders
WW2 Battle of the Bulge - St Vith by Michael Tolhurst
WW2 Battle of the Bulge - Bastogne by Michael Tolhurst
WW2 Channel Islands by George Forty
WW2 Walcheren by Andrew Rawson
WW2 Remagen Bridge by Andrew Rawson

With the continued expansion of the Battleground series a **Battleground Series Club** has been formed to benefit the reader. The purpose of the Club is to keep members informed of new titles and to offer many other reader-benefits. Membership is free and by registering an interest you can help us predict print runs and thus assist us in maintaining the quality and prices at their present levels.

Please call the office 01226 734555, or send your name and address along with a request for more information to:

Battleground Series Club Pen & Sword Books Ltd,
47 Church Street, Barnsley, South Yorkshire S70 2AS

Battleground Europe
NORMANDY

JUNO BEACH
3RD CANADIAN & 79TH ARMOURED DIVISIONS

Tim Saunders

Pen & Sword
MILITARY

This book is dedicated to Stuart Stear much loved and respected member of the family who landed on Juno Beach during the morning of D Day.

Other books in the series by Tim Saunders
Hill 112 – Normandy
Gold Beach-Jig – Normandy
Operation EPSOM – Normandy
Hell's Highway – Market Garden
Nijmegen – Market Garden
The Island – Market Garden

First published in Great Britain in 2004 by
Pen & Sword Military
an imprint of
Pen & Sword Books Ltd
47 Church Street
Barnsley
South Yorkshire
S70 2AS

Copyright © Tim Saunders, 2004

ISBN 1 84415 028 3

The right of Tim Saunders to be identified as Author of the Work
has been asserted by him in accordance with the Copyright, Designs and
Patents Act 1988.
A CIP catalogue record for this book is
available from the British Library
All rights reserved. No part of this book may be reproduced or transmitted in any form or
by any means, electronic or mechanical including photocopying, recording or by any
information storage and retrieval system, without permission from the Publisher in writing.

Typeset in Palatino
Printed and bound in the United Kingdom by CPI
For a complete list of Pen & Sword titles, please contact
Pen & Sword Books Limited
47 Church Street, Barnsley, South Yorkshire, S70 2AS, England
E-mail: enquiries@pen-and-sword.co.uk
Website: www.pen-and-sword.co.uk

CONTENTS

Acknowledgements... 6

Introduction... 7

Chapter 1 THE CANADIANS.................................... 9

Chapter 2 THE ATLANTIC WALL........................... 33

Chapter 3 BOMBARDMENT AND RUN-IN TO THE BEACH............ 49

Chapter 4 THE BEACHHEAD................................... 103

Chapter 5 THE ADVANCE INLAND......................... 119

Chapter 6 ST AUBIN TO LAGRUNE-SUR-MER........ 147

Chapter 7 THE DOUVRES RADAR STATION.......... 165

Chapter 8 THE TOUR OF THE JUNO AREA............. 179

Order of Battle.. 188

Advice.. 189

Index.. 191

Acknowledgements

This book has been a pleasure to write, not least because of Canada's outstandingly positive promotion of projects that serve to commemorate the deeds of Canadian soldiers. This attitude was reflected in the Canadian official and private organizations approached during my research, be they archives, newspapers, regimental museums or associations. It is a shame that similar equally worthy bodies in Britain have been forced, in many cases by under funding, to lower the standards of access and raise increasingly heavy charges for information. I would, however, single out one UK body for particular praise: the British National Archive, the holder of copies of Canadian war diaries, has continued to develop its access policies and is becoming increasingly user friendly. For all those organizations who have contributed to this book, thank you all for your help and encouragement.

I am also grateful to the Juno Beach veterans, both British and Canadian, for taking time to speak to me on a busy D Day anniversary weekend when, with the opening of the new museum at Courseulles, they were very much at the centre of the stage. As usual, the veterans' accounts of their D Day battle on Juno Beach and their attitude to life stand as a source of inspiration for the historian and I have, hopefully, reflected their ethos and approach to battle in these pages.

Anyone who studies the Canadians in the Second World War, must acknowledge the peerless work of Colonel CP Stacey, the Canadian official historian. Wherever a researcher looks, be it in war diaries in Canada or in the British National Archives or in the text of a personal interview or diary, Stacey's familiar pencil marks can be found and the quote is

Colonel CP Stacey

faithfully reproduced in the volumous reports of the Canadian Historical Section.

This book completes the *Battleground* series covering the D Day landing beaches and I am most grateful to Pen & Sword for asking me to finish the D Day line up in time for the Sixtieth Anniversary. Finally, I would point out that even though this book is the last to be published, it is not a reflection of the subject matter or the importance of the part played by the Canadian and British troops who landed on Juno Beach early on 6 June 1944.

Introduction

'When we came off the narrow sandy beach and I saw some Canadian-Scottish lying dead amongst the red poppies. I remembered a poem that we learned in school by Canadian Colonel McCrae: "In Flanders fields the poppies grow Between the crosses row on row". It certainly struck me, seeing them laying dead amongst the poppies blowing in the wind.'

J.H. HAMILTON, ROYAL WINNIPEG RIFLES, CANADIAN 3RD DIVISION

It is not possible to calculate the full scale of the Canadian commitment in men and materials to D Day. Canada's effort was spread across all three Services and not just confined to Juno Beach or indeed the immediate Normandy area. One should also not forget the thousands of excellent CANLOAN officers who were seconded to served with British fighting units. However, with a Canadian division landing in the first assault wave, Juno Beach was undoubtedly the focus of Canadian effort and remains the symbol of the price Canada paid for victory in Europe.

The Royal Canadian Air Force had been fighting in the battle to secure vital air superiority for the invasion force during the months prior to D Day. They had also taken part in the bombing of roads, bridges, and railways in France, Belgium and Holland to reduce the German's ability to reinforce the invasion front. Amongst the first Canadians in action were the men of the Canadian Parachute Battalion who started to drop as a part of 6th Airborne Division before dawn. The Lancasters of Number 6 Bomber Group with their Canadian aircrews followed, dropping tons of explosives on German coastal defences, while above them Canadian fighter pilots scoured the skies for the Luftwaffe. Meanwhile, Canadian piloted fighter-bombers mounted interdiction sorties and struck enemy columns heading towards Normandy and its beaches.

The Royal Canadian Navy's contribution to the invasion fleet consisted of 110 craft of various sizes, crewed by almost 10,000 seamen. Minesweepers led the force south across the English Channel. Canadian destroyers such as HMCS *Algonquin* and HMCS *Sioux* deluged the enemy coastal defences and batteries with fire. The Canadians also provided converted merchant ships such as HMCS *Prince Henry* and *Prince David* to act as troop ships for their fellow countrymen. RCN landing craft flotillas bore the assault force ashore and joined the process of drenching the German defences with fire.

Juno was very much a Canadian beach, with 3rd Canadian Division providing 15,000 of the 24,000 men who landed there during the assault phase and its immediate aftermath. The majority of the remainder were British soldiers, mainly from 79th Armoured Division and the logistic units of 103 Beach Group. Not included in the figure are the Scottish soldiers of 51st Highland Division, who started to land on Juno Beach during the afternoon of D Day. This book is as much about the deeds of the first British troops ashore, as it is about the main burden of fighting that fell on broad Canadian shoulders.

Finally, I wish to point out that I have used the marvellous colloquial names of the three Canadian armoured regiments e.g. The Fort Garry Horse, rather than their official number, 10th Armoured Regiment.

At home or on the ground, enjoy the tours.

Tim Saunders
WARMINSTER 2003

CHAPTER 1

The Canadians

It was on 3 July 1943 that orders started to descend the chain of command from Headquarters First Canadian Army, informing 3rd Canadian Division that they were to begin preparations and training for the Allied invasion of North-West Europe. Lieutenant General McNaughton's letter read:

> 'The 3 Cdn Div has been selected for assault training with a view to taking part in the assault in Operation OVERLORD. The plan for this operation will not be available for some months...'

The selection of a Canadian division for the Assault Phase was both entirely predictable and necessary. The Canadians now formed a significant part of the Allied armies assembling in the United Kingdom and they were the only members of the Allied armies who had direct experience of attacking the German's Atlantic Wall. This experience had been bought at a heavy price, with Canadian bodies littering the shingle of the beach at Dieppe.

The Canadian Army

In the twenty years following 1918, the Canadian Army that had earned the highest reputation in the Great War, amongst both friend and foe alike, had dwindled to a force of a mere 5,000 Regular Army soldiers. Throughout this period, without a military threat to Canada, the Army's main role had become that of 'local police actions in aid of the civil powers'. Even the officer who eventually commanded II Canadian Corps

War is announced to the Canadian people 3 September 1939.

in action, Lieutenant General Guy Symonds, gained a large portion of his experience between the wars commanding operations such as strike breaking. However, Canada's latent military strength lay in its well established, locally recruited, volunteer militia, which had been reconstituted after the Great War under its original names, rather than the anonymous battalion 14-18 war numbers.

The men who were to land with 3rd Canadian Division came from across Canada. There were the Royal Winnipeg Rifles, nicknamed the 'Little Black Devils', the Queen's Own Rifles of Canada from New Brunswick and the Chaudiere Regiment, one of fifteen French Canadian battalions in the Dominion's order of battle. However, the North Shore Regiment was the product of an amalgamation between the wars, of militia battalions who, since Victorian times, had recruited from Canadians of French and Scottish extraction. In contrast, the Cameron Highlanders of Ottawa and the Canadian Scottish had retained their names and clear connections with the old country. The 3rd Canadian Division's full order of battle can be found at the end of the book.

The Canadian Army rapidly mobilized at the outbreak of war in 1939. As in the Great War, the militia soldiers were asked to serve overseas and supplemented by volunteer recruits, the Army's mobilized strength grew quickly. By December 1939, Canadians had started to arrive in Britain with a view to joining the BEF in France, as they had done in the Great War. However, it was apparent that while the men were first rate material, the preparation and training of the division was such, that it would be some

Part of the first contingent of Canadian troops to leave British Columbia for Britain on board a train at Vancouver.

time before the Canadian Division could fully take to the field. Before the division was fully prepared, the fall of France in June 1940 meant that the growing number of Canadians would help to defend Britain in its darkest hour.

As the invasion threat subsided, the emphasis switched to training and the growing number of Canadians became some of the best trained Allied troops in Britain. The First Canadian Army eventually consisted of two corps HQs, two armoured divisions, three infantry divisions and two independent armoured brigades, plus a full array of corps and army support and logistics troops.

After two and a half years in Britain, in mid-1943, I Canadian Corps along with 1st Infantry and 5th Armoured Divisions deployed to the Mediterranean, where they took part in fighting in Sicily and in Italy. While diverting the tough Canadian soldiers away from the invasion of Northern Europe, it did allow the Canadian field army and its commanders to gain vital combat experience. When eventually committed to battle in Normandy, the First Canadian Army and HQ II Canadian Corps usually fought with British and other formations, such as the Polish Armoured Division, in order to flesh-out their order of battle.

Dieppe

'Wednesday, August 19, 1942 – Dieppe. For thousands of Canadians, that was the day stark memory and deep grief were born. It was a day also of full hearted pride. It was a day on which one of the greatest adventures in war's history flared to its height in battle on the French beaches. It was a day that saw tried out the first complete modern experiment in combined operations – which became a fundamental pre-requisite to Allied victory.'

Ross Munro, Canadian Press

Leaving aside the war reporter's patriotic gloss, it is no overstatement to say that what at the time seemed to be a 'terrible reverse' was in fact 'fundamental to success'. The 'costly disaster' that befell 2nd Canadian Division on the beaches of Dieppe, bought vital experience of conducting an assault on the defences of Hitler's Atlantic Wall. The lessons learned, arguably, saved many thousands of lives on the beaches of Normandy in 1944. It is, therefore, important to consider Dieppe's contribution to the plan that the Canadians put into operation on D Day.

Following the success of the St Nazaire raid in destroying a dock capable of berthing a battleship, Admiral Lord Louis Mountbatten tasked his Combined Operations staff to identify a suitable objective for a larger and more ambitious operation. In 1942, Allied and German attention was focused on the development of radar, which was becoming increasingly important to the conduct of the war. It was feared that the Germans had deployed more advanced equipment since the Bruneval raid earlier in the year. However, German radar sites within striking distance of southern England, were very well defended, and thought to be beyond the capabilities of a traditional small raid. One such site was standing on the cliffs just west of Dieppe, seventy-five miles across the Channel from England.

The Dieppe plan, including the participation of the Canadians, was the subject of many debates between the Combined Operations staff and HQ Home Forces. In its final form, the operation was more of a direct attack than a raid, with no fewer than sixteen specific objectives. The objectives, assigned to the commandos and soldiers of the Anglo-Canadian force, ranged from capturing the cliff top radar site in order to enable an expert to examine the German radar, attacking a *Luftwaffe* airfield, to the destruction of militarily useful infrastructure around Dieppe. When questioned about the risks inherent of such an ambitious attack and its place in the war's strategy, Field Marshal Alanbrooke told Churchill that:

'... no responsible general will be associated with any planning for invasion until we have an operation at least the size of an attack on Dieppe behind us to study and base our plans upon.'

In a night assault, Number 3 and Number 4 Commandos would land and take on two batteries of guns that menaced the shipping's approaches to Dieppe. After dawn, two battalions of Canadian infantry would land to the east and west of the port and seize high ground. The main force would land in a frontal assault on the beaches at Dieppe. The whole raid was planned to last around eight hours.

There is insufficient space here to cover the Dieppe Raid in any detail but the operation started to go wrong when, with the force still six miles out to sea, it encountered a German patrol boat. This alerted the enemy. Number 3 Commando's landing failed, while in the main force, there was some confusion and delay before troops landed on Dieppe beach. Elsewhere, there was limited success against strong German ground resistance and air attack. Only Lord Lovat's Number 4 Commando had been completely successful. Anglo-Canadian casualties numbered 3,371, of which, 667 Canadians were killed, 218 were listed as missing and 1,894 were prisoners of war. The Canadian force had consisted of 5,000 men.

The Lessons and Developments After Dieppe

What had gone wrong? First, the Allies questioned their security. Had the German reconnaissance planes seen the amphibious force assembling or had there been a leak from the troops assigned to the raid? Was an operation order allowed to fall into enemy hands? As a result of these questions, in the run up to D Day security became one of the highest considerations; keeping the invasion secret was paramount. Only those who needed to know would be given such information as was essential for

A knocked out Churchill, a burning landing craft and two wounded Canadians on the shingle beach at Dieppe sums up the failure.

their planning. Movement in southern England would be strictly controlled and once briefed, the invasion troops would be kept in quarantine away from the public. In the air above the ports where the assault craft were assembling, the Allied airforces would keep the *Luftwaffe* away.

The intelligence estimate of the German air, naval and land forces that could be mustered in the six hours of the raid had been incomplete but even so, its findings had been largely ignored by troops and commanders who were eager to get into battle. In preparing the D Day plan, establishing air supremacy and carefully calculating the Germans' potential build up of divisions in Normandy were fundamental in establishing the required rate of arrival of follow on forces.

Perhaps the greatest problem revealed by Dieppe was that strong German defences were unlikely to be overcome by surprise alone. General Crerar commented:

> 'Until the evidence of Dieppe proved otherwise, it had been the opinion in the highest command and staff circles in this country that an assault against a heavily defended coast could be carried out on the basis of securing tactical surprise, and without dependence on overwhelming fire support, in the critical phases of closing the beaches and overrunning the beach defenses.'

The response to this problem was the development of a wide range of fire support craft to subdue the enemy's coastal defences. Following their

13

A landing craft tank converted to carry racks of rockets with which to drench the beach with fire.

experience at Dieppe and the news that one of their divisions was to take part in the invasion's initial assault, the Canadians took a leading part in formulating the operational requirement for support craft and tactical doctrine for their employment. A series of exercises in secluded parts of the British Isles were conducted with the new equipment. Ideas were put forward, tested and rejected or earmarked for further development. The resulting fire support craft, that were available in significant numbers on D Day, included up-gunned Landing Craft Gun (LCG), the original version of the 6-pounder armament was replaced by a larger craft, mounting two highly effective 4.7-inch guns. A new weapon designed to 'deluge' the beach defences with fire was a Landing Craft Tank, converted to fire a devastating salvo of high explosive rockets. Earlier versions mounted 792 rounds of 5-inch (36-pound) rockets, while later versions had salvos totalling 1,100 rockets. Their range was 3,500 yards and could 'drench' an area of 750 yards by 150 yards with high explosive. Critical to the effective use of the LCT(R) was the correct positioning of the craft, which was assisted by a simple radar based ranging device. A total of eight LCT(R) were employed against the strong points on Juno Beach.

Another new craft was the 'Hedgerow' conversion of the infantry's diminutive Landing Craft Assault (LCA). This fired twenty-four 60-pound bombs, which were designed to blast a path through barbed wire and mines at the back of the beach. Other special craft included the 'Concrete Buster,' which would engage obstacles and defences in and around German strong points.

One idea to multiply the quantity of fire support available during the run in to the beach that was particularly embraced by the Canadians, was the use of army field artillery firing from landing craft. After a considerable amount of trial, error and technical development, it was found that the ordinary 25-pounder guns could accurately engage targets on a beach out to a range of 12,500 yards. In trials at the Combined Ops Training Centre at Inverrary in Scotland, Canadian gunners demonstrated that they could keep up an impressive rate of overhead fire, yet maintain accuracy. The Canadian official historian recorded that:

'In initial experiments, a battery of guns supported a company of

14

105 mm SP gun, Priest, and its Canadian crew.

infantry and this was gradually increased until several regiments of guns were firing with an infantry Brigade as it landed.'

The development and initial training phases culminated in October 1943 with Exercise PIRATE. Designed to validate the emerging amphibious assault doctrine and tactics, the exercise scenario was based on overcoming the vaunted Atlantic Wall. Central to the exercise's aims was the testing of the integrated fire plan that General Crerar had proposed. Lieutenant Colonel Stacey recalled that 'He emphasized the need for overpowering fire support to get the assault onto the beach and through the defences'. Carrying the Canadian 3rd Division to the exercise assault area on the Dorset coast, was Force J (Juno), which, now renamed, had in fact been the naval task force that had taken the Canadians to Dieppe. A reporter for the Canadian Press, Ross Munro, watched the exercise:

'This highly secret exercise drew most of the senior officers in Britain to Bournemouth to see the Canadians land at Studland Bay. The feature was a demonstration of the new fire support plan.

'It was the newest thing in combined operations and was conceived to be the answer to an opposed landing on a fortified beach. The 3rd Division had developed this fire plan in the months of training. Now it was being displayed for the High Command.

15

'They watched the landing from the headland by Studland Bay. It was done in broad daylight, a significant hint of what was to happen later, and we saw the fleet of several hundred landing craft and the ships carrying the Division come out of Southampton and sail towards the beaches in perfect formation. The destroyers came up and opened fire.

'They pumped shells on to the flat beach; then the Canadian artillery on the landing craft drummed forth with its barrage from the sea. At first, most of the shells fell short but the range was corrected and the beach was showered with bursting high explosives. The rocket craft sailed in towards

Major General Hobart

the shore and did their stuff, hitting the target dead on. Small craft swept the beach with fire from close in and infantry in assault landing craft landed under this curtain of fire, as fighter planes cannoned and machine-gunned dummy pillboxes. It was a minute but accurate demonstration of the D Day plan. Many features had to be tied up and improved, but the great secret was this new conception of devastating fire support from the sea. Everything was to be done to give the infantry more than a fighting chance once they got ashore. Dieppe had clearly shown a need for this.'

Even with land, sea and air firepower integrated to form a powerful rolling blow, the fact that at Dieppe, armour had landed behind the vulnerable infantry and had struggled to get off the beach, was a factor that needed to be addressed.

'Hobart's Funnies' of 79th Armoured division provided the solution. In April 1943, Major General Hobart took command of the Division and, with Combined Operations assistance, studied the experience gained in the Mediterranean and at Dieppe. This he combined with an analysis of the German defences. The result was a series of armoured fighting vehicles or 'funnies' that were manned by men of armoured regiments and the

Duplex Drive (DD) Valentine amphibious tank.

DD Sherman tank with its screen down.

Royal Engineers. Each vehicle was designed to address a specific beach assault problem.

Winston Churchill's enthusiasm for 'gadgets' and technology gave impetus to the development of new weapons, which he encouraged in a Cabinet memo:

'This war is not, however, a war of masses of men hurling masses of shells at each other. It is by devising new weapons and above all by scientific leadership that we shall best cope with the enemy's superior strength.'

Major General Hobart took over development, forging a creative atmosphere and led the work to refine some 'Heath Robinson' designs into effective battlefield weapon systems. In parallel, he developed tactical doctrine for effective use of his 'zoo of funnies'. One of Hobart's first developments was the amphibious tank, capable of landing in the leading wave. The idea of 'swimming tanks' was not new. However, in July 1943 Hobart's demonstration of launching the Duplex Drive Valentine tank from a tank-landing craft persuaded the Chief of the Imperial General Staff to authorise the conversion of 500 valuable Shermans. The key features of this 'funny', were a tall canvas flotation screen and a pair of small propellers that could be driven by the engine instead of the tracks.

Viewing a later exercise at Studland Bay, Montgomery, to the Navy's horror, supported the proposal that the DD tanks were to lead the infantry ashore during the assault. However, these 'unseaworthy craft' with only a low freeboard, were limited to operations in calm seas with a wind strength of less than Force 4. 79th Armoured Division trained ten armoured regiments to use the DD tanks at Stokes Bay on the Solent and on various Scottish lochs. These regiments included the Canadian 1st Hussars and the Fort Garry Horse, who were to lead 3rd Canadian Division ashore. Lieutenant Little of the Fort Garry Horse described his first encounter with a DD tank:

Badge of the 79th Armoured Division

'This little barge turned and headed towards us, and as it rolled you could see it touch the bottom of the lake and started to roll up. This was a tremendous surprise. Then as it rolled forward the tracks kept coming higher; and then as it got to the edge of the water, down came the screen and there was the gun. This was a surprise and a shock.'

The Allies went to extraordinary lengths to ensure secrecy, so that the German defenders would share Lieutenant Little's surprise and shock.

AVRE with its Petard Demolition Gun.

Most numerous of the 'funnies' were the Armoured Vehicles Royal Engineer (AVRE). A conversion of the heavily armoured Churchill Tank, the AVREs' main weapon was a Petard Demolition Gun

Two pictures from a series showing an AVRE crossing a small section of mock Atlantic wall, using a small box girdar bridge and a Chepsale fascine.

that fired a 40-pound projectile, known as a 'Flying Dustbin', out to a range of 200 metres. The gun's shaped charge warhead, most accurate at a range of eighty metres, was designed to take on steel and concrete defences on the coast of France. A variety of obstacle crossing devices could be carried on the back of the AVRE. The most commonly used was a fascine of logs for dropping in anti-tank ditches or craters.

Another version of the AVRE was a vehicle mounting a device for placing charges against sea walls built by the Germans. The Royal Engineers carried out much of the development work on training areas in Hampshire. A piece of 'Atlantic Wall' was built on Hankley Common (near Aldershot) that can still be seen today, along with breaches made in it by the AVREs during trials.

Twenty year old Lance Corporal Stuart Stear of the Royal Engineers, who was to land on Juno Beach with the Canadians, described seeing a series of encouraging exercises:

'In 1944, 619 Company was based in Troon, Scotland and nearby at Mocham Loch we built a replica of the Atlantic Wall. It took us a month to

A Sherman flail tank, specifically designed for mine clearance, and dubbed the 'crab'.

Flamethrowing tank known as the Crocodile.

> *pour the concrete and complete the building work and not nearly so long for Hobart's Funnies of 79th Armoured Division to literally smash it up. It gave us a lot of confidence to see how quickly their great big demolition guns destroyed it and to watch the infantry and DD tanks practising coming ashore.'*

Completing the line-up of new vehicles were the Crab and the Crocodile. With resistance organizations reporting that the Germans were laying more and more mines along the coast, and appreciating how slow and ponderous conventional mine clearance was, a quicker less vulnerable method had to be developed. Again under Hobart's direction, the unreliable Matilda Scorpion, as used at El Alamein, was developed on a Sherman chassis into a successful operational vehicle. The Crab or Sherman Flail, mounted a revolving drum with heavy chains that beat the ground, setting off mines and ripping up wire as it advanced at 10 MPH. Second Lieutenant Ian Hamerton had envisaged 'elegant armoured advances across the plains of Europe' when he joined the 22nd Dragoons. He was disabused of this traditional notion during a visit by General Hobart:

> *'You have been chosen to sweep away all the mines in front of the army.' There was a silence as we pondered unenthusiastically the role of minesweepers. Hobo left behind him a sad and disillusioned collection of men. No sweeping across the fields of France in our cruiser tanks – just sweeping mines.'*

Unglamorous maybe but crewing a flail was a vital task that did much to help the Canadians get off Juno Beach and through the Atlantic Wall.

The Crocodile was a flame thrower conversion of a standard Churchill tank. Towing a 400 gallon armoured trailer, the Crocodile could squirt a lance of flame a hundred yards long, at a rate of four gallons a second. The result was a fearsome weapon system but as it was delivered only just before the invasion, few troops of the assault divisions knew about the Crocodile and little use was made of flame on D Day, despite numerous suitable targets.

The divisional historian recorded that up to the last moment challenges to the 79th's technical inventiveness were received.

'An unexpected difficulty appeared a few weeks before D Day. A very daring reconnaissance confirmed a fear hitherto only hinted at by geologists – some beaches [including Mike Sector of Juno Beach] *had strips of a peculiarly soft blue clay, in which all vehicles would bog. A geologically similar beach was found at Brancaster in Norfolk and a special trials wing had to be very quickly established... to evolve solutions to this new problem.*

'As a result a proportion of the AVREs were equipped with Bobbins on which were wound coir and tubular scaffolding carpets laid by the AVRE as it advanced up the beach. By means of these carpets, the Crabs and tanks would be able to ascend the beach and sand dunes.'

The final lesson of Dieppe was that some officers attributed the failure to 'bad luck'. However, Allied Combined Operations staff were determined, in the time available before the invasion, to make their own good luck, with some highly detailed planning of the enormous undertaking that lay ahead.

Training and Preparation

3rd Canadian Division had been training hard for the invasion since the autumn of 1943. The following quotes from General Keller's weekly progress report to Canada dated 22 January 1944 give a flavour of the preparations.

'North. Shore Regt, who represented this Division at a Marching and Shooting competition, will carry out a six day trek commencing 24 Jan. The trek will include field firing at Canford Heath (including 3-inch mortars) and street fighting in Southampton. ... 7 Cdn Brigade: Combined Ops training both dryshod and with craft, continued. ... Regiment de Chaudiere carried out further training in clearing booby traps. 2 Cdn Armoured Brigade's range firing will take place at Lydd from 24-30 Jan.'

While the assault troops were training, others were making technical preparations. Lieutenant General Morgan described another essential aspect of training and preparations before more ambitious exercises could be undertaken:

'... every single vehicle that is to be discharged on to a beach must be waterproofed, that is so protected that it will suffer minimum harm from immersion in the sea to a depth of some feet ... for instance, a Jeep could be driven along the seabed with nothing protruding above the surface but the drivers head and a few inches of air intake pipe'.

Lance Corporal Stear was amongst the many soldiers who had to learn the

Canadian 3 inch mortar crew – Training early 1944

techniques for covering his vehicle's electrics with specially developed, colour coded, material made from grease and asbestos fibres. The process included the fitting of extension pipes and specially manufactured splash plates. In this aspect of assault landing preparations, the British and Canadians were at a disadvantage. They had over one hundred different types of non-armoured fighting vehicles and engines in service compared to only twelve in the US inventory:

> 'My first amphibious landing training was a vehicle-waterproofing course at Warminster on Salisbury Plain. Here we were taught how to fit extensions to exhausts and engine breathing pipes to enable vehicles to drive from the landing craft onto the beach. Our final exam was to drive the vehicles down a ramp into a tank full of water, to test the sealing of the plugs in the vehicle hull. If you drove through successfully, you passed but if your vehicle stopped in the tank, you were sent back to keep practising!'

With D Day approaching, exercise followed exercise, as all aspects of the coming invasion were practised. The 3rd Canadian Division embarked at

Southampton and from the small ports of the Isle of Wight and set out for the amphibious exercise SODAMINT, which took place at Bracklesham Bay and Selsey Bill. According to the exercise intelligence summary, the small coastal town of Emsworth was held by the German 582 Grenadier Regiment. The 'Germans' were in fact being played by British Home Guard and troops from holding units who were earmarked as battle casualty replacements for D Day.

The final exercise, even though it wasn't known as such until much later, was Exercise FABIUS III. It took place in early May. The Canadians used almost the exact D Day landing tables and practised the operation from embarkation through the assault, to the setting up of the beach organization. The smooth flow of entries in the battle log indicate that the exercise, with its multitude of components, went according to plan and units reported steady well organized progress.

With training complete, final preparations were under way. The routine of the last few weeks was broken by a series of visits by 'Distinguished Visitors' to 3rd Canadian Division. On 13 May, General Eisenhower visited 9 Cdn Brigade at Rooksbury Camp where, according to the war diary he was greeted by the Brigade's massed pipe bands under Pipe Major Corsterphine of the Highland Light Infantry of Canada. Amongst other visitors the 3rd Division was the Right Honourable WLM King, Prime Minister of Canada who met all officers and Senior NCOs on 18 May. On 20 May, Montgomery addressed the division's senior officers at a Southampton Girls Grammar School amidst great security.

A Canadian infantry platoon photographed in a Landing Craft Assault during Exercise FABIUS III.

D Day Plans

At the Casablanca Conference in January 1943, Churchill and Roosevelt ordered the formation of a combined military staff, under Lieutenant General Morgan. As Chief of Staff to Supreme Allied Commander (COSSAC) he was to plan Operation OVERLORD, the invasion of North-West Europe. The scale and depth of planning and the preparation required to break through Hitler's vaunted Atlantic Wall was unprecedented in military history. However, even this plan to assault the Normandy coast, was expanded by General Montgomery on his return from the Mediterranean. In his Presentation of Plans at HQ 21st Army Group, on 7th April 1944, Montgomery explained that he had lengthened the frontage of the Allied assault to sixty miles by increasing the number of landing beaches to five. The amphibious landings were to be preceded by the insertion of three airborne divisions on the flanks of the invasion area. His logic was that with a longer frontage the Germans would be less able to concentrate their forces for a decisive counter attack against the Allied beachhead.

1st British Corps was to command the landings at Sword and Juno Beaches and, therefore, took operational control of 3rd Canadian Division until such time as the Canadian II Corps HQ came ashore at about D+20. XXX Corps was to land at Gold Beach, spearheaded by a single division, the US V Corps on Omaha Beach and VII Corps on the Cotentin Peninsula at Utah Beach. Further troops were to land behind the assault troops on D Day's second tide. A 21st Army Group memo recorded that 'Success is dependent on speed; speed in overcoming opposition to the initial landing, and speed in getting ashore a follow up and build up force superior to anything the enemy can bring against it.'

Lieutenant General Crocker's I Corps Operation Order gave an overview of the Anglo-Canadian part of the Allies' Overlord plan:

> 'Second Army is assaulting with I and XXX Corps through beaches between Port en Bessin and the Orne with the object of securing and developing the bridgehead south of the line Caumont – Caen and SE of Caen in order to secure airfield sites and to protect the flank of First US Army.'

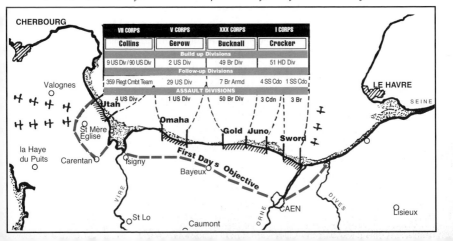

**Lieutenant General
Sir John Crocker**

'After completion of landing of I and XXX Corps, VIII And XII Corps are landing in succession.'

The same document went on to give the Corps mission and method to be employed:

'I Corps will assault the beaches between Graye-sur-Mer and Ouisterham and will advance to secure, on D Day, a covering position on the General line Putot en Bessin – Caen – thence R Orne to the sea, preparatory to a subsequent advance south and SE.

Method

'I Corps will assault, 3 Cdn Inf Div Right, two bdes up; 3 Br Inf Div Left, one bde up. The tasks of the assaulting divs are to break through the coastal defences and advance some 10 miles inland on D Day. It will be the task of these divs to secure the covering position...

'Great speed and boldness will be required to achieve this. It will be necessary to forestall the action of the enemy's local reserves quickly, to overcome minor resistance met with during the advance, to get set before the arrival of reserve formations, and be ready to meet the enemy's first counter attacks, which must be expected to develop by the evening of D Day.

'As soon as the beach defences have been penetrated therefore, not a moment must be lost in beginning the advance inland. Armour should be used boldly from the start. Such action will forestall the enemy's reaction, confuse him, magnify his fears and enable ground to be made quickly.

'All available artillery must be ready to support the advance. If opposition is met which can not be overcome by these strong advance guards, simple plans embodying the full resources of the artillery and armour must be employed to dislodge the enemy quickly and certainly '

3rd Canadian Division's Plans

7 Cdn Brigade recorded in its war diary that on 14 May the 'Div Op O was received'. Brigade Commander and Brigade Major spent all day 'reading in'. Major General Keller's orders were, however, not only for his Canadian infantrymen but for his fellow countrymen in 2 Armoured Brigade and a whole host of British units, mainly the 'funnies' of 79th Armoured Division and elements of 103 Beach Group. This force totalled some 24,000 men of which 61 percent were Canadian. The divisional operation order gave General Keller's D Day mission.

'10.   3 Cdn Inf Div, with under comd, 2 Cdn Armd Bde and 4 SS

24

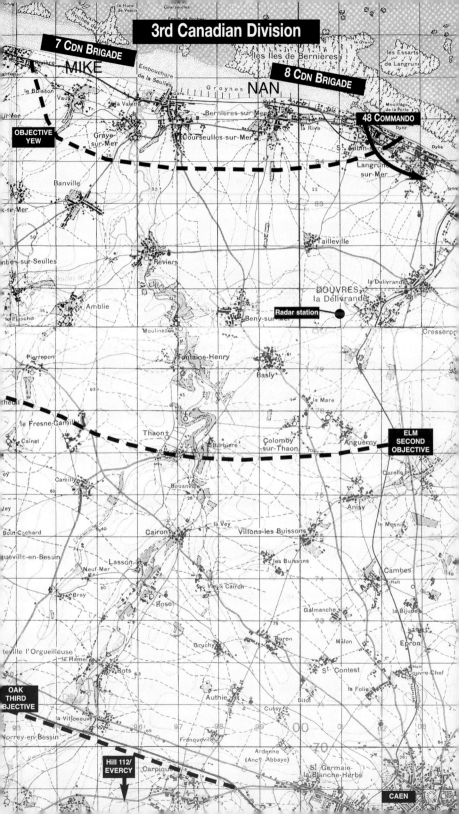

[Special Service – commando] *Bde less two commandos, is to assault between GRAYE-SUR_MER and LAGRUNE-SUR-MER and is to adv and secure on D Day a covering position on the gen line PUTOT EN BESSION – CARPIQUET- to road and railway bridge 995682* [Outskirts of Caen].'

Having landed astride the small but well defended port of Courseulles, in common with other division's D Day tasks, 3rd Canadian Division's objective lay almost ten miles inland from Juno Beach. It would be difficult to reach and in the event proved to be more than a little optimistic. The operation order goes on to divide the operation into code named phases and allocate troops to task:

'11. (a) *3 Cdn Inf Div is to assault on a two bde front through MIKE and NAN sectors. It is to be done in four phases:-*

PHASE 1 – *Assault and capture beachhead YEW.*

PHASE II – *Capture the intermediate objective ELM.*

PHASE III – *Capture of the Final objective OAK*

PHASE IV – *(D plus 1) Reorganization of the final objective.*

'(b)   *The assault is to be done with:*

RIGHT [MIKE] – *7 Cdn Inf Bde Group – two battalions up with under command 6 Cdn   Armd Regt.*

LEFT [NAN] – *8 Cdn Inf Bde Group – two battalions up with under command 10 Cdn Armd Regt.*

RESERVE – *9 Cdn Inf Bde Group with under command 27 Cdn Armd Regt.*'

9 Cdn Brigade had two landing options; Plans A – Mike Sector and Plan B – Nan Sector. Depending on circumstances, General Keller reserved the option, which was not available on any other D Day beach, to switch the landing of his follow up brigade to either of his two sectors. 2 Cdn Armoured Brigade, as its operation order detailed a 'Special task':

'INTENTION

26. *2 Cdn Armd Bde will sp 3 Cdn Inf Div onto the final objective OAK and will be prepared to adv on   afternoon of D Day to secure the high ground at EVRECY.*'

This task has often been taken as a firm requirement. However, the following sentence from the operation order makes it clear that this was a contingency plan:

'32. *Should serious enemy resistance fail to develop on D Day, 2 Cdn Armd Bde with under command* [an all arms group of armour, artillery, infantry and engineers] *will adv to secure the high ground at EVRECY. C Sqn Inns of Court* [Yeomanry – Corps recce regiment] *will probably be placed under command. Their tasks included the blowing of bridges over the River Orne and acting as a base for subsequent operations.*'

The 'BIGOT Top Secret' D Day plans were released down the chain of command and the men who were to carry them out spent a nervous few weeks contemplating the obstacles and defences that they were to be pitted against. Major Fulton of the Royal Winnipeg Rifles, who was 'Bigoted' or let into the invasion plan during in May 1944, wrote:

'Once we were made aware of where the invasion was to take place, the next thing was to find out all we could about the beach defences and the troops that manned them... Every day prior to D Day we received new air photos of the beaches. Every morning we studied them diligently looking for any new beach obstacles which could change our plans.'

The Juno Beach H Hour

Amongst the lessons of the trials and exercises was the fact that with so many different craft, all with different speeds and characteristics, it would be impossible to muster them all in assault formation in the dark. Therefore, for this simple practical reason, it was determined from an early stage that the assault would need to be some time after dawn. Supporting this decision was the need for accurate air and naval bombardment, which would be better achieved in daylight. The combination of good moonlight for parachute operations and bombing, along with the correct state of tides shortly after dawn, limited OVERLORD to two windows of opportunity, both of only a few days per month.

Each of the assault beaches had its own practical problems that dictated the exact time of landing. Due to the time lag in the tide flooding in from the Atlantic, H Hour for the landings on the British beaches was to be fifty-five minutes later than those on Omaha and Utah Beaches. However, air photograph interpreters noted that the rocks off Juno's Nan Sector did not appear to be covered by the incoming tide as predicted. The Navy defended the accuracy of their charts but visual evidence won the day and H Hour on Nan Sector was delayed by twenty minutes to 0745 hours and, in order not to have a vastly different H Hour, by ten minutes to 0735 hours in Mike Sector. These adjustments proved to have been unnecessary, as it was subsequently found that the data on the naval charts was correct and that the 'rocks' seen on air photographs were in fact, beds of six foot long seaweed! However, in the event, the actual H Hour on Mike and Nan Beaches was governed by delays in the arrival of some elements of Force J.

Embarkation and the Weather

The plan to embark 3rd Division efficiently and quickly was, if anything, more complicated than the actual landing plan. Delivering troops, with their vehicles, stores and equipment to the correct landing craft in the reverse order to the assault was a piece of, largely unrecognized, detailed staff work by the Combined Operations planners. Despite the heavy training commitments, the Royal Navy had ensured that

97.3 per of the 4,000 plus landing ships and craft of various types were serviceable at the beginning of June 1944, negating much last minute 'hot planning'. While overhead, the Royal Air Force kept enemy aircraft away from the south coast, 3rd Canadian Division moved via a number of marshalling and staging areas around Portsmouth and Southampton. From here, they moved in carefully planned convoys to embarkation points in ports and the smaller harbours along the Solent and on the Isle of Wight.

Royal Engineer Lance Corporal Stuart Stear was amongst those bound for Juno Beach:

> *'As D Day approached, we moved down to a tented camp in the New Forest and then on to a concentration camp near Southampton where we were sealed in prior to embarkation, which took place on about 4 June 1944. We drove our truck across the specially built concrete hard and once on board our American LCT, we moved out into the Solent and anchored off the Isle of Wight. There were thousands of ships all of different size around us.'*

The 'sausage machine' started on 30 May. Assault paraphernalia, including life belts, sea sickness tablets and sick bags, was issued to all men along with their pay in French Francs, which finally confirmed that their destination would be France. The fact that it all went so smoothly is a testament to the thorough organization and the repeated practices to which both troops and locals had become familiar.

Out in the Solent, Canadian Press reporter Ross Munro, had been assigned to the Canadian Headquarters aboard HMS *Hilary*.

> *'Staff officers of the 1st Corps and the 3rd Canadian Division were aboard now and they had little to do but await the start of the battle they were to direct. The plan was fixed and nothing could alter it.*
>
> *'But the weather would dictate whether the attack could be made or not and the wind was still whipping down the Solent from the white-capped Channel. Even in the lee of the land the sea was rough and the small craft clustered around us tossed sickeningly. Finally, the signal was flashed to the invasion fleet: "Twenty-four hours postponement."*
>
> *'It was dismal news ... [but] "If we can't do it tomorrow, we'll do it the next day or the day after that," said Major Bill Seamark, who was on the divisional staff. 'We have four or five days leeway now – that is, the tides will still be okay for that period – and if the weather is completely impossible there will be a postponement for a few weeks until the tides are right again. But the attack is going in."*
>
> *'We went up on deck every few hours to look at the sea. The wind did not abate. The rumors started. A gale was sweeping in from the Atlantic ... ships were being swamped in the Channel, a Spitfire pilot reported the sea quite calm near the French coast, so the grapevine reports ran.'*

However, for the ordinary soldiers waiting on the cramped craft, with little

Packs including air photographs and maps were circulated amongst the soldiers waiting on the landing craft. Compare the detail shown on the map and photograph of Courseulles.

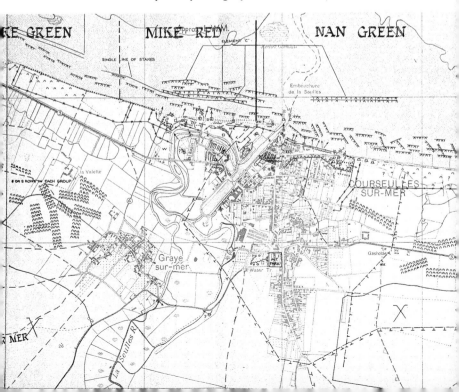

Southwick House.

information on which to base rumours, time weighed heavily. Lance Corporal Stear recalled:

'We were sharing the LCT with the French Canadians of the Chaudiere Regiment [8 Canadian Brigade] and some Shermans on the lower deck. To pass the time the Canadians taught us to play a dice game called Shoot. There was nothing else to do and I lost all my invasion money but it kept my mind off the invasion.'

A short distance away, on the northern outskirts of Portsmouth, General Eisenhower had a difficult decision to make. Assembled with his staff in Southwick House, the Supreme Commander pondered '...the big question'; the weather that would prevail during the only period of early June that we could use, the 5th, 6th and 7th.

Group Captain Stagg.

'We met with the Meteorlogic Committee twice daily, once at 9.30 in the evening and once at 4 in the morning. The committee ... was headed by a dour but canny Scot, Group Captain JM Stagg. At these meetings every bit of evidence was carefully presented, carefully analysed by the experts and carefully considered by the assembled commanders. With the approach of the critical period the tension continued to mount as the prospects for decent weather became worse and worse...

'At 3.30 the next morning [4 June], our little camp was shaking and shuddering under a wind of almost hurricane proportions and the accompanying rain seemed to be travelling in horizontal streaks. ... in such conditions there wasn't any reason for even discussing the situation.'

However, the following day, at the 2130 hours meeting, Group Captain Stagg reported:

'Gentlemen, since I presented the forecast last evening some rapid and unexpected developments have occurred over the north Atlantic. In particular a vigorous cold front from one of the depressions has been pushed more quickly and much further south than could have been foreseen. This front is approaching Portsmouth now and will pass through all Channel areas tonight or early tomorrow. After the strong winds and low cloud associated with that front have moved through there will be a brief period of improved weather from Monday afternoon...

'Admiral Creasey put the first question after a rather prolonged silence. "Is there a chance that conditions over Wednesday to Friday could be better than you have pictured them to us?"

'Air Chief Marshal Tedder then asked, "What confidence have you in the forecast you have given us?" "I am quite confident that a fair interval will follow tonight's front. Beyond that I can only repeat that the rates of development and speeds of movements of depressions in the Atlantic have

30

been exceptional for the time of year.

'...Both Air Chief Marshal Leigh Mallory and General de Guingand questioned me further about the details of cloudiness expected overnight Monday/Tuesday. Admiral Ramsay said "If OVERLORD is to proceed on Tuesday, I must issue provisional warnings to my forces within the next half-hour". Air Chief Marshal Leigh Mallory was still anxious about the effectiveness of his heavy bombers. ... Some of his colleagues seemed to think this was an unnecessarily pessimistic view, but Air Chief Marshal Tedder supported Leigh Mallory: "Yes, the operations of the heavy and medium bombers will probably be a bit chancy." General Eisenhower put the question directly to General Montgomery: "Do you see any reason why we should not go on Tuesday?" Montgomery's reply was immediate and emphatic: "No, I would say – go!"*

'... the Supreme Commander started his summing up: "After hearing all your views, I'm quite certain we must give the order for Tuesday morning. Is there any dissenting voice ...?".'

Supreme Commander General Eisenhower.

At 0415 hours on 5 June 1944, the Supreme Commander, with a look of confidence in his eyes, said 'Ok lets go'. The D-Day assault was on.

The assembled Allied commanders and staff left Southwick House and returned to their own headquarters and issued orders for OVERLORD to begin. Eisenhower returned to his tactical headquarters (codenamed Sharpener) in Sawyer's Wood less than a mile from Southwick. Here, General Eisenhower wrote a short speech which he was to broadcast in the event of the assault failing. In his script, he accepted full blame for failure. However, a few hours later a smiling, light-hearted and outwardly confident Supreme Commander was bidding farewell to his airborne troops.

By 0445 hours, the signal confirming that D Day was on had been flashed to Commodore Oliver aboard HMS *Hilary*. With radio silence in force, boats went from ship to ship around Force J, passing the welcome news that D Day was on. Once breakfast was complete, as recounted by Lieutenant Colonel Stacey, the troops opened their:

'... sealed parcels of maps were broken open and final briefing began. Bogus names and coordinates were exchanged for genuine ones. Troops spent their remaining time cleaning weapons. On such occasions, messages were read to the troops from the Supreme Commander, from General Montgomery and General Crerar.'

Aboard their Landing Ship Infantry (LSI), the departure of the Highland Light Infantry of Canada (HLI of C) seemed almost routine. Their war diary recorded:

'... There were no bands or cheering crowds to give us a send off on the

31

biggest military operation in history. A few dockworkers silently waved goodbye. Friends called farewell and bon voyage from one craft to another. A few craft blew their whistles and up on the bridge Sagan the piper played 'The Road to the Isles.

'...There were craft of every type imaginable, there were blunt nosed LCTs butting their way along, small LCIs riding the crests like corks, big channel packets with their LCAs lashed to their sides and proud cruisers running hither and yon in search of an enemy who would dare to poke his head out of the water. In the distance big 'battle wagons' lent an air of confidence and security to the scene. The 9th [Canadian]'Highland' Brigade was on its way.'

FIRST CANADIAN ARMY

A PERSONAL MESSAGE
FROM
LT-GEN H. D. G. CRERAR, C.B., D.S.O.,
GOC-in-C, FIRST CDN ARMY

It is not possible for me to speak to each one of you, but by means of this personal message, I want all ranks of the Canadian Army to know what is in my mind, as the hour approaches when we go forward into battle.

I have complete confidence in our ability to meet the tests which lie ahead. We are excellently trained and equipped. The quality of both senior and junior leadership is of the highest. As Canadians, we inherit military characteristics which were feared by the enemy in the last Great War. They will be still more feared before this war terminates.

The Canadian formations in the assault landing will have a vital part to play. The plans, the preparations, the methods and the technique, which will be employed, are based on knowledge and experience, bought and paid for by 2 Canadian Division at DIEPPE. The contribution of that hazardous operation cannot be over-estimated. It will prove to have been the essential prelude to our forthcoming and final success.

We enter into this decisive phase of the war with full faith in our cause, with calm confidence in our abilities and with grim determination to finish quickly and unmistakably this job we came overseas to do.

As in 1918, the Canadians, in Italy and in North West Europe, will hit the enemy again and again, until at some not distant time, the converging Allied Armies link together and we will be rejoined, in Victory, with our comrades of I Canadian Corps.

To be read to all troops.   (H. D. G. Crerar) Lt-Gen

Chapter 2

The Atlantic Wall

'I have received a warning that invasion will be launched between the 3rd and the 10th. I should perhaps add, gentlemen, that we have received similar warnings every full-moon period and every no-moon period since April.'

GENERAL RICHTER, 716TH INFANTRY DIVISION

Without doubt, the much-hyped Atlantic Wall was not as strong as Goebbels's propaganda would have the German people or the Allies believe. However, in June 1944, it did present a serious obstacle to the Allies that, with every passing day, grew stronger. But on the night of 5 June, the German defences were at a low state of readiness. Unlike the Allied meteorologists, the Germans predicted marginal weather; they had interpreted met reports from U-Boats in the Atlantic slightly differently. The weather conditions, combined with the assessment that the state of the tide was wrong for an Allied landing, led to the invaders gaining a considerable degree of tactical surprise. Colonel von Luck of 21st Panzer Division explained:

'The general weather conditions worked out every day by naval meteorologists and passed on to us by Division, gave the all clear for 5 and 6 June. So we did not anticipate any landings, for heavy seas, storms, and low flying clouds would make large operations at sea and in the air impossible for our opponents.'

Rommel took the opportunity to travel to Germany to see his wife and to plead with Hitler for the forward deployment of armour. In Normandy, senior officers were travelling south for a map exercise. The soldiers in the strong points (*Wiederstandneste*) were on minimum manning and much of 21st Panzer Division was deployed on blank firing night exercises.

German Operational Strategy in the West

When it became clear to Hitler that Operation BARBAROSSA had frozen to a halt within sight of Moscow in late 1941, he issued instructions to build a wall along the coast of Europe. By March 1942, this had been translated into Fuhrer Order Number Forty. The important section read:

'The coastline of Europe will, in the coming months, be subject to the danger of enemy landings in force... Even enemy landings with limited objectives can seriously interfere with our own plans if they result in the enemy gaining a toehold on the coast... Enemy forces that have landed must be destroyed or thrown back into the sea by immediate counter attack.'

33

The focus of German work was to continue strengthening port defences and surrounding areas as *Oberefehlshaber* (OB) West assessed that an invading force could not be sustained without the use of a major port. The Pas de Calais, with its ports, and proximity to Southern England was heavily defended, due to the Allied advantages of a relatively long 'time over target' for aircraft and quick turn around for shipping. Elsewhere along the 3,000 miles of coastline from the North Cape of Norway to the Pyrenees Mountains, a thin, patchy, string of defences began to take shape. Starved of human and material resources, work on the Atlantic Wall was slow but with Allied success in the Mediterranean and growing Allied strength in the west, Hitler issued Fuhrer Order Number Fifty-one in late 1943:

> *'All signs point to an offensive on the Western Front no later than spring, and perhaps earlier.*
>
> *'For that reason, I can no longer justify the further weakening of the West in favour of other theatres of war. I have therefore decided to strengthen the defences in the West, particularly at places where we shall launch our long-range war* [V-weapon] *against England. For those are the very points at which the enemy must and will attack: there – unless all indications are misleading – the decisive invasion battle will be fought.'*

Along with the new orders came a new commander. At the same time as Montgomery and Eisenhower were returning from the Mediterranean,

Generalfeldmarschall Rommel and Hitler.

Generaleldmarschall Rommel took up the post of Inspector General of the Atlantic Wall. His responsibilities extended beyond his own Army Group B in Northern France to cover the Atlantic and the North Sea coasts. What he saw did not impress him, despite the best efforts of the Todt labour organization and its much-publicised works around the Pas de Calais. Building on his experience of operating against an enemy with air superiority in the Mediterranean, Rommel assessed that he would have to defeat the Allied invasion on the beaches. To that end, with incredible vigour, Rommel set

Many captured weapons were used on the Atlantic wall. In this case a Dutch manufactured Lewis gun provides anti-aircraft cover.

about constructing what he called a 'devils garden' of defences. He drove his soldiers and workers hard and in many places, despite supply difficulties, they worked in shifts twenty-four hours a day. A priority was providing overhead cover to the gun batteries, which involved the building of massive reinforced concrete casemates. This was a slow process but by 6 June, most artillery and anti-tank guns were casemated.

In six months the Germans laid the majority of the 1.2 million tons of steel and poured the 17.3 million cubic yards of concrete used in construction of the Atlantic Wall which produced a hard crust of mutually supporting defended localities. All along the coast, these localities were surrounded by over four million anti-tank and anti-personnel mines, while on the beaches, 500,000 obstacles of various types were built.

Hitler had created a command system in the west with overlapping areas of responsibility, which was an elastic web rather than a taught chain

The obstacles as envisioned by Rommel – another Dieppe.

German Atlantic Wall anti-aircraft gunners relax awaiting their next kill – note the silhouettes painted on the wall.

of command. This led to a loss of unity of command but within Commander in Chief West's armies, *Generalfeldmarschall* von Rundstedt

Generalfeldmarschall von Rundstedt

and his generals agreed on the necessity of a well defended coastline. However, they could not agree on how to use the scant German armoured reserves in France. With little firm intelligence to rely on, von Rundstedt supported by the senior panzer officers advocated the conventional military option of identifying the main enemy attack before massing reserves to counter-attack. Rommel, however, had experienced the power of the Allied air forces, and consequently, doubted the ability of the panzer divisions to assemble and make a timely move to battle while subjected to Allied air interdiction sorties. Rather than having the panzer divisions located in the centre of France, Rommel advocated forward locations from which the panzers could strike the Allies as soon as they had landed. He argued that 'penny packeting', which is contrary to the credo of any armoured

36

commander, would in fact deliver vital armoured counter-attacks at the crucial time and place early in the battle while the Allies struggled to establish a beachhead. However, the senior panzer commanders, with their Eastern Front experience, disagreed and both sides vigorously lobbied Hitler. The result was that the Führer insisted that his personal authority was required before any panzer formation was redeployed or committed to battle. Even so, Rommel successfully used his influence to argue the case for control of three of the eight panzer formations in the west, with the remainder split between *Panzergruppe* West and the SS's 1st SS Panzer Corps. It is no wonder that von Rundstedt complained 'As C-in-C West, the only authority I had was to change the guard at my front gate'. Canadian intelligence officer, Major Milton Shulman, having studied the German chain of command, wrote:

> 'When the invasion began there was, therefore, neither enough armour to push the Allies back off the beaches in the first few hours, nor was there an adequate striking force to act as an armoured reserve later on. No better design for a successful Allied landing could have been achieved than this failure to concentrate the armour in the West along one unified and determined course.'

Deception

Winston Churchill wrote: 'In war-time, truth is so precious that she should always be attended by a bodyguard of lies.' In order to protect the OVERLORD plans and prevent the Germans from feeling they could concentrate against the Normandy beachhead, Operation BODYGUARD was set up by the Allies. BODYGUARD proved to be one of the most comprehensive and successful deception and counter-espionage operations ever undertaken in the history of warfare. Anthony Cave Brown described the operation's aim:

> 'Plan Bodyguard, and the intricate special means that would be employed in its execution, had been designed for a single purpose – to enable the best and finest young men to get ashore – and stay ashore – in the first tumultuous hours of D-Day.'

BODYGUARD also sought to stop the Germans from realising their reinforcement potential of some thirteen divisions by D Day plus five. It was important that as many enemy divisions as possible remained guarding other sectors of the coast against a second landing.

Operation BODYGUARD sought to persuade Hitler and his staff to identify a series of strategic considerations. Firstly, that the Allies thought that the bomber offensive may be sufficient to bring Germany to her knees i.e. a lack of commitment to a Second Front. Secondly, to keep the German garrisons in Norway, South-Eastern Europe and the Mediterranean fixed in place and away from Northern France. Thirdly, that the invasion would be

Hitler was becoming increasingly concerned about Normandy as a possibility for the expected Allied invasion.

co-ordinated to start after the Russian summer offensive and finally, BODYGUARD sought to mislead the Germans about the size and location of the Allied invasion forces.

This last aim was the most important and with German agents either eliminated or turned, the Allies set about reinforcing the German belief that they would invade the continent at the Pas de Calais. The component Operation, FORTITUDE (South), was a masterpiece of deception that was still effective well after the Allies had broken out of Normandy. Lieutenant General Morgan (COSSAC) described FORTITUDE's aim and some of the difficulties:

> '... there was always the need to do everything possible to induce the enemy to make faulty dispositions of his reserves, to strive if possible to have him at a disadvantage. ...One bogus impression in the enemy's mind has to be succeeded by another equally bogus. There had to be an unbroken plausibility about it all, and ever present must be the aim, which was to arrange that the eventual blow would come where the enemy least expected it, when he least expected it, and with a force altogether outside his calculation.'

The very core of Operation FORTITUDE was the creation of a fictitious First US Army Group (FUSAG) in South-East England under the flamboyant General George Patton. To convince the Germans that the

Allies had many more divisions than they actually had available, a combination of 'special means' were used. Chief amongst these was the use of double agents, such as the Spaniard Garbo, who fed details of fictitious formations and troop movements to Berlin. While in south-east England, a small number of British and American signallers created FUSAG's electronic signature by simulating their training and administrative radio traffic. The signallers were supported by a few genuine troops and numerous poorly camouflaged dummy tanks and landing craft and, finally, General Patton's newsworthy presence. So successful was FORTITUDE that in March 1944 German military intelligence, the *Abwehr*, was reporting that FUSAG:

> '... contains three armies each of three corps, totalling twenty-three Divisions, amongst which, the location of only one need be regarded as questionable. The report confirms our operational picture.'

The Germans finally believed that there were eighty-five to ninety Allied divisions assembling in Britain, together with seven airborne divisions. In fact, the Allies had only thirty-five divisions, including four airborne divisions. By the time D Day came, this estimate had found its way into all the *Wehrmacht's* enemy information charts and from there into its operational level plans. The Allied deception was so successful partly because it was in von Rundstedt's interest to inflate the number of divisions that he was likely to face to secure as many troops as possible for the defence of the west.

Despite FORTITUDE, Hitler was becoming increasingly concerned about Normandy and urged von Rundstedt to move troops to its defence.

A rather idealistic view of the inside of a Atlantic Wall troop shelter.

Generalmajor
Wilhelm Richter
commanding
716th Coastal
Division.

Germans –
mine laying
as part of the
defences.

General Warlimont of OKH explained,

>'We generals calculated along the lines of our regular, military education, but Hitler came to his own decision, as he always did, on his intuition alone'.

In this case, Hitler's intuition was too late and the picture painted by BODYGUARD and FORTITUDE was so widely accepted that there was little that could be done in the time available to redeploy significant forces to Normandy.

German Coastal Defences

General Richter's 716th Coastal Division, under command of LXXXIV Corps, held the lower Normandy coast. The 716th had been raised during May 1941 and had been deployed to Normandy in June 1942 in response to Hitler's Führer Order Number Forty. It was formed with soldiers largely below the age of eighteen and with men over thirty-five. However, the best of the younger soldiers had been regularly taken as drafts for the Eastern Front and were replaced with 'boys' and soldiers who had partly recovered from wounds or had suffered third degree frostbite during the Russian winter. Over fifty percent of the division were eventually categorized as being of a low physical grade and the division's ration return for May 1944 gave a strength of only 7,771 men.

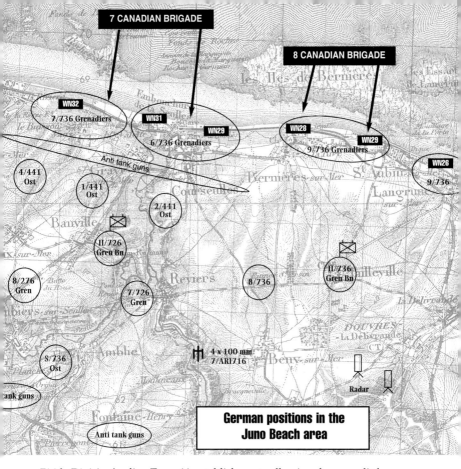

German positions in the Juno Beach area

716th Division's slim Type 44 establishment, allowing for very little equipment or transport, was designed for manning static positions. For two years, with scant resources, the division held a seventy mile front between the River Dives in the east at Carbourg, through to the base of the Cotentin Peninsular. However, on 15 March 1944, Hitler's intuition came into play and LXXXIV Corps inserted the newly organized and trained, 352nd Division into the coastal defences. This 'field quality' division took over the defences between Le Hamel (Jig Sector of Gold Beach) and the mouth of the Vire River (between Omaha and Utah). This placed Juno Beach in the very centre of 716th Coastal Division's shortened sector. Extensive regrouping of regiments, battalions and even companies took place between the 716th and 352nd Divisions. In a post-war debrief, 'it was discovered from General Richter of 716th Division that 726 Infantry Regiment, less one battalion had been placed under command of 352nd Division from 716th Division'. The net effect of these moves was to considerably thicken up the defences. Initially the defences occupied by the redeployed troops were field defences around platoon strong points, which were typically upgraded to company or at least two platoon strength. Allied intelligence only picked up the first hints of the

Osttruppen **under command of 736 Regiment receive a briefing on a sandtable model.**

redeployment and 352nd Division's move forward on 14 May 1944 but by then it was too late to alter plans.

In the Juno Beach area, 716th Division had deployed four reinforced infantry companies in the coastal strong points. Covering what was to become Mike Sector was 7 Kompanie, 6/736 held the defences of Couseulles, while 5/736 occupied the strong points in Bernieres 5/736 Grenadiers (Nan Sector), with a fourth company, 9/736 Grenadiers and St Aubin. Just to the east, in the Lagrune area, which the commandos were to clear, were elements of 9/736 Regiment. Included amongst the coastal defences were several platoons of *Osttruppen* (Russian prisoners of war co-opted into the *Wehrmacht*, *Osttruppen* were also to be found in the artillery batteries at Ver-sur-Mer and at Beny-sur-Mer. These batteries were respectively captured 100mm Czechoslovakian and French 155mm guns.

About a mile inland from the coast a second line of field fortifications had been created by troops released by the insertion of 352nd Division. In this new line the 716th Division had four companies of German soldiers and at least two companies of *Osttruppen*. Behind this position, there were few reserves and such reserves as were available, were held well back and had to cover the entire division's frontage. There was little armour available to General Richter, but Number 1 *Kompanie*, 716 *Panzerjager*

Battalion had approximately ten self-propelled assault 75mm guns (Pak 40s), mounted on the chassis of obsolescent French tanks captured in 1940. Located near Bayeux, these assault guns were earmarked for immediate counter-attacks. On D Day, they spent the day marching and counter-marching on LXXXIV *Korps* Orders as German commanders' perception of the threat changed. All the while they were under attack by Allied fighter-bombers.

Rommel had, by a slight of hand, managed to deploy at least one armoured formation, 21st Panzer Division, closer to the coast than officially approved. Located south-east of Caen the panzers formed a potentially powerful operational reserve that could strike against Sword and Juno Beaches by midday.

Much has been written debating the relative difficulty of the tasks faced by Allied troops on various beaches. What is without doubt is that the well defended harbour of Courseulles in the centre of it and with a string of coastal towns to the east, 3rd Canadian Division had some potentially strong defensive positions to take. However, the coastal troops holding these positions were not generally of the same field quality as those faced by the Americans at Omaha and 231 Brigade on the western portion of Gold Beach. The 3rd Canadian Division's Intsum described the qualities of the enemy troops in 716th Division:

> 'This division, like others in the 700 series, is a low category division of two regiments of infantry and one regiment of artillery (two field and one medium battery). All personnel are trained in coast defence although the better trained have been transferred to field divisions. The remainder consists of young soldiers, men of older classes unfit for service on the Eastern Front and men who have been wounded and are only slightly disabled. In comparison with a first class field infantry division, its fighting value has been assessed as 40% in a static role and 15% in a counter attack. The division should be up to strength in personnel and equipment ... it has been reported that non-German soldiers, Russians, Monguls, etc. have been seen in the divisional area ...'

In another post war interrogation, the Chief of Staff of 352nd Division, *Oberstleutenant* Fritz Ziegelman, confirmed this assessment of the coastal troops' quality:

> 'In taking over the sector, we were surprised that the reinforced 726th Grenadier Regiment was very backward in its training, because of the continuous supply of troops to new formations, and a lack of initiative in the officers and NCOs in training the remainder. In addition, the corps of NCOs was composed of elements which hoped to survive the war without having been under fire.'

Oberstleutenant Ziegelman's impression of the quality of the coastal troops is confirmed by the confession of one of their battalion commanders,

Oberstleutenant Pflocksch, who held positions in St Aubin: 'I asked myself whether I should be happy or unhappy about the invasion and I found out there was every reason to be somewhat happy. Now the war will very soon come to an end.'

As already indicated, the quality of the German troops garrisoning the Atlantic Wall was further reduced by the practice of incorporating prisoners of war from the Eastern Front into the *Wehrmacht*. *Osttruppen* recruitment had followed months when:

> *'Twenty to thirty men died every night due to the combination of hours of hauling wood, generous lashing with leather whips, and bad food.*
>
> *'Suddenly, in early 1942 ... Barracks were cleaned, men deloused and food became more abundant. For six weeks they were forced to take exercise so they could get their strength back. ... In May 1942 they discovered they were now part of four Armenian battalions which were being formed and trained to fight in the German Army.'*

By D Day approximately 75,000 *Osttruppen* were serving with the German Army in France, mostly as rear area troops. *Generalfeldmarschall* von Rundstedt was not impressed with their qualities, 'The Russians constituted a menace and a nuisance to operations'. However, according to General *der Infanterie* Gunther Blumentritt, of the operational *Ost* battalions:

> *'...only four remained with LXXXIV Infantry Corps, and only two of these were committed on the coastal front. One battalion, which was especially noted for its trustworthiness, was committed on the left wing of 716th Infantry Division, at the request of this division.'*

This battalion, 441 *Ost* Battalion was positioned on the Meuvaines Ridge, on 716th Division's left flank in the area of the British Gold Beach, with a company inland from Juno. 439 *Ost* Battalion was mainly deployed with 352nd Division but 3 *Kompanie* 642 *Ost* Battalion was in the second line some two miles inland from Sword beach. In addition, recent German research has confirmed that both 726 and 736 Regiment had troops attached from the four *Kompanie*s of 439 *Ost* Battalion. These soldiers were normally attached to German units in platoon strength to boost the overall number of defenders in a specific location and would account for the fact that many of the prisoners taken were of an eastern appearance. It would also be wrong to dismiss *Osttruppen* as entirely worthless, some did fight well, including a group on Juno Beach who resisted capture until the evening of D Day and some did not surrender until D+1.

In summary, the enemy on Juno Beach were not of the highest quality but they had been in position for a long time and mostly had concrete shelters and casemates, which were clear force multipliers. The German regrouping of platoons and companies made it difficult for Allied intelligence to calculate the number of defenders and, as a consequence,

Albert Speer head of the Todt Organization and architect of the Atlantic Wall.

Todt workers constructing concrete casemates on the Channel coast.

German soldiers inland from the Juno area indicate to the camera where they would rather be... Paris.

Keeping a watch on the Channel.

the Canadians faced significantly more enemy troops in the coastal defences than had been expected.

The *Wiederstandneste* (WN)

It must have been of considerable concern to Major General Keller to have the defences of Courseulles (WN 29-31), in the centre of Juno Beach. Other than the major defences around the small port, every thousand yards or so, amongst the dunes and coastal villages, there were strong points (*wiederstandeste*). Although each German strong point differed according to its task, the Canadian operation order gives a very good summary:

> 'The coast is held by a system of linear defences arranged in strongpoints. A company area consists of several strongpoints occupied by either one section, two sections or in some cases one whole platoon.

> 'Each battalion has three companies forward with support weapons sub-allotted down to sections, there is therefore probably no battalion reserve. Each strongpoint may however be expected to have an immediate reserve within the position.

> 'Defences consist mainly of pillboxes and open machine gun positions with open emplacements for 75 mm guns reinforcing the stronger positions. Strongpoints are usually set astride exits to cover the beaches with enfilade fire. In addition it can be assumed that each platoon will have a 2 inch (50 mm) mortar, and that a total of six 3-inch (81 mm) mortars per battalion will be shared out to particular strongpoints. . . . Each strongpoint is surrounded by a protective minefield and wire as well as the minefield and wire on the [back of the] beaches.'

46

Beach Defences

While the quality of the coastal troops of 716th Division was questionable, they were deployed in a relatively strongly held stretch of the coastline. In front of Rommel's strong points and their belts of protective wire and minefields were the open expanses of the beaches, covered by the strong point's interlocking arcs of fire. The Germans had assumed that Allies would land on a rising tide, nearing high water, in order to reduce the distance across the exposed beach. Therefore, a 'devils garden' of beach obstacles, designed to impede a landing at high water, had been deployed in rows between twelve and seventeen feet above the low-tide mark.

Much of the material used in constructing beach obstacles was recycled from old border fortifications of the occupied countries. Czech hedgehogs (jagged steel stakes), curved girders from the Maginot Line and even steel gates from the Belgian fortresses, would on a rising tide, be a test of the Royal Navy and Royal Marine landing craft crew's seamanship.

Gefreiter Werner Beibst describes the work of a coastal infantryman:

'One of our main duties was to keep guard in two-and-a-half-hour shifts, throughout the day and night, just looking at the sea. There were occasionally bombing raids. Then there was Rommel's idea – I heard later that it had come from him – to fell trees, pines or some other kind of trees that grew abundantly in that area. These were to become 'Rommel's Asparagus'. Anyway, it was our job to fell these trees and then horses were used to drag the trunks out of the woods, back to the coast. Then we had to wait for the tide to go out to plant the trees really far out on the sand. All this we did more or less without any kind of mechanical help. It was terribly difficult work and required huge numbers of people. Once the trees had been erected, mines were planted on the seaward side of the trees. This was all intended to catch the landing craft that we expected to land in that area. We spent April doing this work.*

'We were really strained by the work. During the day, we worked felling and dragging the tree trunks and then at night we had constant watch, such that we could never really sleep properly. We were all quite young at the time, seventeen or eighteen years old, and we really needed our sleep and decent food, but got neither. The bunkers were frightfully primitive, sometimes they were only earth bunkers and we had to live in them; the bombing raids made it impossible to live any other way.In our bunker there were eight men sharing; sometimes it was twelve and very restrictive and unpleasant. No one could move and the sleeping-bunk, well, it was not unlike being in a submarine. Washing arrangements were very primitive and we could never take our clothes off to sleep because we had to keep our uniforms and our boots on at night.*

'I was really only properly scared during the bombing raids. Sometimes they happened during the day, when we were out on the beach, fully* *exposed, erecting these Rommel Asparagus in the sand. When the raids came, all we could do was throw ourselves down in the sand. A number of people in my group were actually killed on these occasions.'*

Conclusion

It is a fact that defensive positions can always be improved. However, after six months as Inspector of the Atlantic Wall, Rommel felt he had made significant progress. True, the German coastal defences were still a crust and work on the inland defences was only just being made possible by the arrivals of formations such as 352nd Division. In addition, the panzer divisions were, in Rommel's view, badly located. However, Rommel wrote to his wife in early May, 'I am more confident than ever before. If the British give us just two more weeks, I won't have any more doubt about it'. Finally, just ten days before D Day, Rommel issued a Special Order of the Day, which reflected his own growing confidence in the outcome of an Allied assault on the Atlantic Wall.

'I have expressed my deep appreciation of the well-planned and well-executed work performed in so few months.

'The main defence zone on the coast is strongly fortified and well manned; there are large tactical and operational reserves in the area. Thousands of pieces of artillery, anti-tank guns, rocket projectiles and flame-throwers await the enemy; millions of mines under water and on land lie in wait for him. In spite of the enemy's great air superiority, we can face coming events with the greatest Confidence.'

ROMMEL *Generalfeldmarshal*, 22 May 44

The weather in early June that had so concerned the Allied commanders brought a certainty to the Germans that the invasion would not take place in such conditions; after all, *Kreigsmarine* minelayers had been driven back into port by the heavy seas and strong winds. *Oberst* Zimmermann commented that 'there seemed no prospect of an immediate assault against this sector of the coast'. All along the Normandy coast the defences went to 'minimum manning' and unit commanders took the opportunity to exercise their men or simply let them rest.

As a result of the weather and deception measures, the Allied attack on the Atlantic Wall was going to achieve tactical surprise.

Chapter 3

Bombardment and Run-in to the Beach

With the Juno Beach Bombardment Force, already at sea, HMS *Hilary*, Commodore Oliver's Force J Flagship, weighed anchor in the Solent and led the Force, with its cargo of assault troops out into the Channel towards Assembly Area Z. Located off the Isle of Wight, the Allied flotillas met in accordance with the carefully coordinated Operation NEPTUNE naval instructions, before heading south to Normandy.

Seaman Francis Hynes aboard Landing Craft Flack (LCF) 36 recorded:

> 'The fleet moved out into the very choppy sea. Thousands of vessels of varying size and shapes, some sporting barrage balloons as protection against low-flying attacking air forces. It was a bad long cold night; attempts were made to supply drinks to the men on very small assault craft; for the most part, it was merely a sympathetic gesture. The sea was covered in ships just as a leopard with measles is covered in spots.'

Aboard their by now familiar transports, the Anglo-Canadian assault troops destined for Juno Beach, settled down to sleep as best as they could. Seasickness (despite the issue pills) for some and nervous anticipation for many, made it an unrestful night. While the assault troops tried to sleep, the British, Canadian and US ships' companies of Force J were very much awake and alert. At his Battle Headquarters at Southwick House, Admiral

HMS *Hilary* riding at anchor prior to the attack on the Normandy coast.

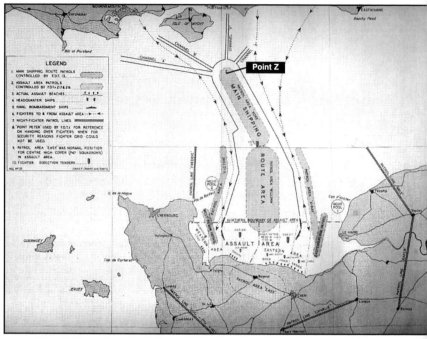

The D Day air cover plan.

Admiral Ramsey

Ramsey waited impatiently. He wrote:

'There was an air of unreality during the passage of the assault forces across the Channel. The achievement of strategic surprise was always hoped for in NEPTUNE but was by no means certain, whereas that of tactical surprise had always seemed extremely unlikely. As our forces approached the French coast without a murmur from the enemy or from our own radio, the realization that almost complete surprise had been achieved.'

Below decks, after an uncomfortable night in his American LCT, Royal Engineer Lance Corporal Stuart Stear recalled:

'The crossing wasn't too rough but breakfast was a bit strange for our taste – porridge with bacon and sausage stuck in it! There was nothing else so we ate it.'

For the Infantry of the Queen's Own Rifles of Canada, as recorded in their war diary:

'D Day begins with very early reveille – spirits are very high but naturally one can feel the nervous tension in the air. Unfortunately, the water is still quite rough. Breakfast is served and all men who wish it are given a good shot of good old Navy rum.'

As the force closed in on the Normandy coast, a sleepless reporter, Ross Munro, went up on HMS *Hilary's* deck:

'... the wind howled through the wireless masts which sprouted profusely from the upper deck. The sky was black as the inside of a gun

barrel and spray and rain lashed the deck. It was a terrible night for the crossing. The sea seemed worse than ever and the ship creaked and groaned as she ploughed her way through it.

'The Algonquin *just astern of us was a blob in the night and you could barely pick out the silhouettes of other ships near us in this curtain of darkness... The night was ominously quiet, apart from the elements...*

'Occasionally there was a great flash over the French coast as RAF heavy bombers struck at gun positions in the le Havre area. A number of those big guns had a range of twenty miles. Some star shells arched into the sky.'

At 0558 hours, HMS *Hilary* came to anchor some seven to eight miles from Juno Beach. Major General Keller had joined the Commodore on the bridge before dawn and scanned the coastline ahead with the watchkeeper's binoculars. The only evidence of action was the flicker of shellfire and the ricochets of tracer rounds well to the east and off to the west. Clearly, the Allied airborne divisions were in action. As time passed, across their front, the commanders could see the flash of exploding bombs and naval shells as the principal batteries were engaged.

At this point, it became evident that four of Force J groups, including the LCTs of Force J1 carrying 7 Cdn Brigade's AVREs, had during the night entered a swept channel further to the west than the ones intended. This took some time to correct and bring errant LCT back to their proper place behind the craft carrying the DD tanks. They were not the only offenders. The official historian recorded that,

Major General Keller

'... *the tardiness of certain groups caused both Assault Group Captains to defer H Hour for a further ten minutes. It was thus decided that the times for H Hour should be 0745 hours for 7 Cdn Brigade (Mike and Nan Green Sectors) and 0755 hours for 8 Cdn Brigade (Nan White and Red Sectors)'.*

He concluded that,

'It was not a happy situation for it meant that the swiftly rising tide, aggravated by heavy seas, would render the [enemy's beach] obstacles inaccessible all the sooner'.

This decision was circulated around Force J shortly after 0634 hours when radio silence was broken by a periodic call by HQ ships.

A variety of converted coasters, now categorized as Landing Ship Infantry (LSI), had anchored around HMS *Hilary*. Landing Craft Assault (LCAs) were lowered from the LSIs' davits, while some unlucky assault troops had to climb down scramble nets into the diminutive craft. The wind was estimated as being force five to six and the wave height three to four feet. The LCAs pitched and tossed alongside their mother ships as the force assembled. This weather, at the very edge of practicality for

51

Force J heading for the French coast.

amphibious operations in 1944, made for an uncomfortable run in to the beach.

Captain 'Nobby' Clarke recounted how he watched his soldiers sitting in the landing craft:

'I was very interested in the expressions on their faces. Some looked like 'wounded spaniels', some were quite nonchalant, others made a feeble show of gaiety. What amused me most was a fat boy trying to whistle, but the best he could do was blow air with a squeak now and then. ... I was pretty scared.'

Private Hamilton and his platoon of the Royal Winnipeg Rifles had other things to distract them along with the misery of sea sickness:

'We were fortunate because from [LSI] Langleby Castle, we were directly lowered by davits from the ship. The water was much more choppy

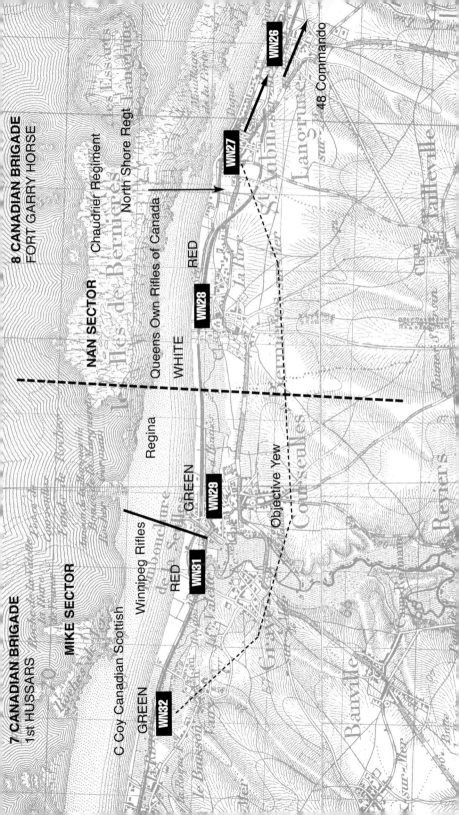

German gunners manning a 50mm anti-tank gun inside a casemate.

than we had ever encountered in any of our schemes, and coming off the mother ship a large wave hit our landing craft and as we swung back, we came in at an angle and were slightly damaged at the back. One of the twin engines was knocked out, and when we did hit the water, we were short of power. We were some six miles out from the beach at that time, and our sailors had quite a job getting us in to the shore.

'Because of lack of power, we were being swamped by heavy waves. The waves were so high, they were washing over our landing craft, and our first casualty was Rifleman Munch, who was, as we all were, very, very seasick. He was lying on the gunwale and as we came in to about two miles offshore, a large wave washed him off, and he went down. We never saw him again.'

Meanwhile, the Germans defenders had been called to their battle positions before dawn and it was not long before the soldiers of 716th Division realized that they were directly in the path of the Allied invasion. Grenadier Christian Hubbne in his post in *Wiederstandnest* 28 on Nan Beach wrote:

'We slept in a bunker not far from the shore and went to bed as usual that night. But soon after five o'clock we were roused by our Sergeant-Major who yelled that an enemy fleet was off shore and we must get to our

battle stations at once. We rushed about in great confusion and fear, trying
to eat something and drink coffee while pulling on our equipment. It took
us almost fifteen minutes to reach our position in a fortified bunker, which
included machine-gun posts overlooking the beach.

'I will never forget our first sight of that invasion fleet. The horizon was
filled with ships of all kinds and of course huge battleships all lined up in
the grey light of dawn. We were amazed and frightened; we had never seen
anything like it and wondered how we could possibly repel such an armada.
Of course, there was no sign of our own navy or Luftwaffe and we felt
betrayed! Our Sergeant tried to steady our nerves, but I could see he was as
amazed as we were. Then our Lieutenant came to remind us of all the drills
we had done and not to fire until the enemy was in the water and at their
most vulnerable. We knew all that, but wondered if we would still be alive
to act at all.'

Grenadier Hubbne and his fellow soldiers of 736 Grenadier Regiment did
not have long to wait before the great guns of the Fleet swung towards
Juno Beach.

The Bombardment

RAF Bomber Command and the USAAF 8th Airforce had begun the
bombardment of the Normandy coast some weeks before D Day. The focus
of their attacks had to be concealed from the Germans, by spreading the
bombing effort along the entire coastline, with only one in three raids being
directed against targets in Normandy. The attackers included Number 6
Group, which consisted entirely of Royal Canadian Air Force Halifax and
Lancaster bomber squadrons.

Bomb damage was inflicted on the *Wiederstandneste* and German
records indicate that it slowed construction and that they had to regularly
repair the field defences and trenches that connected the concrete
casemates. This took manpower that could otherwise have been used in
thickening up minefields or placing additional beach obstacles. British
naval officer, Lieutenant Wiliamson, questioned a German prisoner of war
aboard an LCI on the evening of D Day:

'He told me that "We were accustomed to attacks by your bombers but
we were always warned and were in shelter". Looking around at our fleet
he shook his head and added, "but for this fire, we were totally unprepared.
No man could stand up to it".'

On the night of 5 June, the RAF and their Canadian counterparts,
concentrated on bombing the main German naval and artillery batteries
along the invasion coast. In the Juno area, bombing priority was given to
the strong points at Courseulles (WN 29 and WN 31) and Bernières (WN
28), while those at St Aubin (WN 27) and Lagrune (WN 26) were afforded
second priority.

The main D Day fire plan began at 0552 hours, when the cruisers HMS *Belfast* (twelve 6-inch guns) and HMS *Diadem* (eight 5.2-inch guns) opened fire. While scoring few direct hits with map predicted fire at their inland targets, the 223 rounds fired by *Diadem* neutralized the four 105mm guns in the Beny-sur-Mer battery during engagements at 0552, 0725 and 0905 hours The guns of eleven destroyers, including those of the Canadian ships *Algonquin* and *Souix*, joined the bombardment, as Force J approached the enemy coastline. Although they did not know it at the time, the Navy scored an early success, when they successfully engaged, via an air observation post aircraft, 8 *Kompanie* 736 Grenadier Regiment. These troops, who should have been sheltering in their field defences of the second line, inland from Juno Beach, had been seen searching for non-existent paratroopers and suffered heavy casualties. Consequently, 8/736 Grenadiers were dispersed and did not play a significant part until late in the afternoon of D Day.

When the main naval bombardment checked fire for fifteen minutes, before resuming to cover the assault force's final run-in, the German defenders were struck again by the Allied airmen. This time it was the medium and fighter-bombers. Their job, while avoiding cratering the beach and creating additional underwater obstacles for both infantry and armour, was to attack the strong points. The weather made the task of the medium bombers difficult and, as a result, some of their bomb load fell

An A20 Havoc of the USAAF 8th Air Force passing over the invasion fleet after a raid on the German defences.

amongst the fields and villages behind the beach. However, the rocket firing Typhoons were able to strike with accuracy right up to the last minute, with one aircraft even being unluckily struck by a pattern of rockets that had just been fired by a Royal Navy LCT(R) during the final run-in to the beach.

At 0715 hours, the Royal Canadian Artillery's amphibious guns, which they had done so much to develop, opened fire from the LCTs. Royal Canadian Signals officer, Major Patterson described the action of the four artillery regiments, each equipped with twenty-four 105mm guns:

'Range[ing fire], with smoke began at 10,000 yards and fire for effect at 9,000 yards, timed so as to commence at H minus 30 minutes. From then until ... a range of 2,000 yards each gun fired 3 rounds every 200 yards. The total HE expenditure at H plus 5 minutes was thus 105 rounds per gun.

'At this point, the LCTs did not continue on their course in order to touch down and off load the guns, for the beach was not yet ready to receive them. Instead, they turned off to a flank to a waiting position... On landing they deployed and went into action as quickly as possible.

'To complete this picture, it is necessary to envisage 24 LCT approaching shore, each craft carrying four guns (one troop). The total volume of fire from these 96 guns would equal 10,080 rounds. The fall of shot was to be observed and controlled by Forward Observation Officers travelling in advance of the assault waves...

'Each regiment was to bring down a concentration on one of the four principal strongpoints in 'Juno' sector, i.e., those at Courseulles (on either side of the breakwater), at Bernières and St. Aubin, ending just as the leading infantry touched down. These four regimental concentrations were thus designed to complement the fire delivered against the same targets by LCT (R.). But it must be emphasized that their effect was to be neutralizing, not destructive. Neither sufficient weight nor accuracy to achieve penetration of concrete defences could be expected of field artillery afloat.'

As planned, the eight Landing Craft Tank (Rocket), split between Mike and Nan Sectors, fired their salvo of rockets as the leading flights of landing craft approached the beaches, deluging the four main German Wiederstandneste with fire. Finally, the 'Hedgerow' craft engaged the beaches and its immediate defences with high explosive, while the 'concrete busters' targeted the enemy casemates. This brought the noise of howling shells, the throb of marine and aero-engines, exploding rockets and the crack of small arms fire to a mind-shattering crescendo.

Grenadier Christian Hubbne, who had been called from his shelter at dawn to man his position, was on the receiving end of the bombardment:

'Sure enough not long after that the terrible bombardment began and it went on and on. We had not expected anything like it and cowered in our holes waiting to be buried alive or blown to bits. The great shells from the

DIAGRAM SHOWING ESSENTIAL ELEMENTS OF ONE BRIGADE GROUP APPROACHING THE BEACH

A schematic example of a brigade landing based on one brigade's landing on NAN Beach.

battleships made a fantastic noise and the ground shook when they detonated. We guessed that all the seafront houses and our defences were being smashed. The bombardment seemed to go on for a very long time and all the while the air was also filled with the sound of bombers hammering away at us.

'Then, at last the noise seemed to lessen and our Sergeant told us to stand-to as the enemy were about to land, so we jumped to our weapons, trembling with fear and from the effects of the bombardment. One of the units on our left was composed of Eastern 'volunteers' from Russia, I believe, who looked very Asiatic in appearance; I wondered if they had survived and would surrender at once.

'Then we could see the enemy landing craft coming in to the shore and the warships still firing. We forced ourselves to get ready.'

8 Canadian Brigade Group – Nan White and Red Sectors

Having formed up, the LCAs of Force J2, with 8 Cdn Brigade aboard, headed for Nan Sector. However, Commodore Oliver wrote in his post-operational report: 'The final approaches of the Assault Force to the beaches was far from the orderly sequence of groups and timing which had been the rule during exercises.' In the worst case, one company of infantry had not received the order delaying H Hour, continued shoreward and were only recalled when they were a few hundreds of yards from the beach. However, the fire plan went well and the escort destroyers headed for the flanks of the flotilla of landing craft. From these positions, as close in as 3,000 yards, the destroyers engaged targets on and to the flanks of the landing beaches. BBC correspondent Colin Wills was watching. Perhaps he was unaware of the landing craft flotilla's co-ordination difficulties but it was not the job of a reporter of the day to highlight negative points.

'Hello BBC! This is Colin Wills recording on board an infantry landing craft on June 6th 1944. ...we are moving towards the shore, the battleships and other bombardment ships over on the flank are pouring in their fire and now other warships, moving up front in our path, are laying a smoke screen and now there is a signal from the flagship: "All hands to beaching stations." ... We have started our run-in to shore – we are still some distance out but I may be able to report a little bit more of the landing.

'This is the day and this is the hour! The sky is lightening, lightening over the coast of Europe, as we go in. ... along the shore there is a dense smoke screen as the battleships and the smaller warships sweep along there, firing all the time against the shore. The sun is blazing down brightly now; it is almost like an omen the way it has suddenly come out just as we were going in.

'There go the other landing craft past us. Some are left behind, the slower ones, each taking their part and going in at the right time for their right job. ... There is an enormous cloud of smoke along the shore, not only

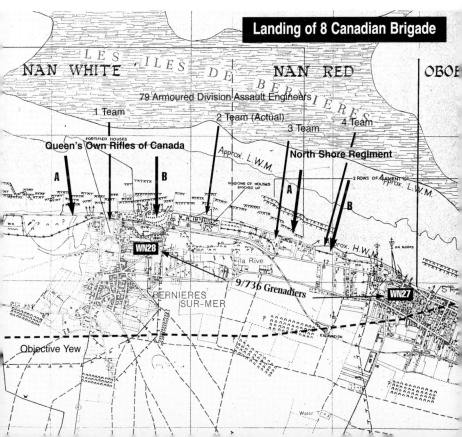

from the smoke screen but from the terrific bombardment. All the ships are blazing away now. All around this great grey-green circle of water there are ships, ships moving in, ships on patrol, ships circling, ships standing-to and firing. We are passing close by a cruiser, a cruiser that has been taking part in the bombardment but is now, I imagine, on some sort of general patrol.

'... I can't record any more now because the time has come for me to get my kit on my back and step off on that shore and it's a great day.'

Well ahead of Colin Wills were the AVREs and other specialist assault armour of 79th Armoured Division. The state of the sea was such that the DD tanks of the Fort Garry Horse, which should have swum ashore five minutes ahead of them, were ordered to be landed direct from the LCTs with the infantry. However, in the event, the DD tanks touched down on parts of Nan Sector, behind the leading wave of infantry, at about 0815.

According to Commander Eastern Task Force, Admiral Vivian, enemy fire at the leading flight of landing craft 'began to manifest itself at 3,000 yards from the beach and even then fire was only desultory and inaccurate'. Clearly, the fire plan had at this point neutralized the defender's capability to respond effectively. As the landing craft approached the beach they could see that the belt of obstacles was almost covered by the tide and consequently they represented a highly dangerous and 'unpleasant prospect for the landing craft crews'. Admiral Vivian wrote of his J2 Group landing craft crews of, many of whom struck mines:

'Their spirit and seamanship alike rose to meet the greatness of the hour and they pressed forward, over or through mined obstacles in high heart and resolution; there was no faltering and many of the smaller Landing Craft were driven on until they foundered.'

Despite the severe losses amongst Royal Navy and Royal Marines crewmen manning bow stations, casualties amongst the assault troops were relatively light.

LCTs carrying the assault teams of 79th Division, Centaur tanks of the Royal Marine Assault Regiment and Canadian field engineers were leading. They started to land on Nan Sector at 0805 hours, or twenty minutes later than their deferred H Hour. The first flight of LCTs included the flail tanks of B Squadron 22 Dragoons and the AVREs and armoured bulldozers of 80 Assault Squadron RE. They were divided into four breaching teams, each equipped with a mix of six vehicles organized to deal with the particular obstacles and defences that faced them at their landing point. Once ashore, they were to blast their way through the obstacles creating an exit or lane off the beach for the DD tanks, infantry and their support vehicles. Meanwhile, the Royal Canadian Engineers were to remain on the beach attempting to clear the rapidly sumerging obstacles. However, the delay in landing meant that they were not able to achieve a great deal, despite their valiant efforts.

Holding the coastal defences that 'Hobart's Funnies' and the Canadians attacked where approximately two German infantry companies deployed on a front of almost three miles. *Wiederstandnest* 28 at Bernières and smaller defended localities in the surrounding area were held by 5 *Kompanie* 736 Grenadier Regiment (5/736 Gr Regt), while the strong point at St Aubin (WN 27) was held by 9/736 Grenadier Regiment. The defences were known to be centred on 50mm anti-tank guns, machine guns and mortars, all in concrete casemates, which were linked up by a network of revetted trenches. The positions were surrounded by barbed wire entanglements and minefields extended into the surrounding fields and dunes. Some of the villas and houses behind the beach had been strengthened and fortified as additional defensive positions.

Bernières – Nan White Sector

The 79th Division's history describes the landing and what, for most of the armoured vehicle crews, was their first battle:

'Number 1 Team touched down exactly as planned but late, and the leading Crab flailed up to the sea wall followed by an AVRE which laid its bridge. The first AVRE across hit a mine and blocked the gap: it was later bulldozed aside and the lane cleared by hand. The bulldozer driver was killed by a mine. The two Crabs in the team then cleared another path up to a place where the sea wall was half broken – this they mounted and continued flailing as far as the first lateral. Here they turned and joined the two exits, then cleared a lateral lane as far as No. 2 gap. First one fascine and later a second was dropped into the ditch across the road – this was later bulldozed into a good crossing place. The late touch-down had meant that the beach was already crowded with infantry who severely limited Petard operations: fortunately neither strong opposition nor a heavily mined beach were encountered although between the top of the beach and the road, mines were found in plenty and included Teller and anti-personnel types...

'Number 2 Team was driven off its course by other craft and beached about 300 yards east of their target. They were at once engaged by 50-mm fire from the right: the Bridge AVRE was hit and another AVRE commander killed: one of these guns later fell to a 'Dustbin'. The 12 foot sea wall was only about 50 yards away and Crabs flailed up to it. Petards, of which two were out of action, failed to make sufficient gap and the crater caused was soft and steep. Meanwhile the infantry led the way to a beach ramp blocked by Element C. These were demolished by Petard fire, the Crabs flailed up the ramp; one was caught in wire but was freed under cover of smoke, the ditch was filled by a fascine and the lane, at last, through to the road. A second gap was later made to by-pass Bernières.'

An officer with the 22 Dragoons, Lieutenant Ian Hammerton, was the flail troop commander landing with Number 2 Team. He wrote:

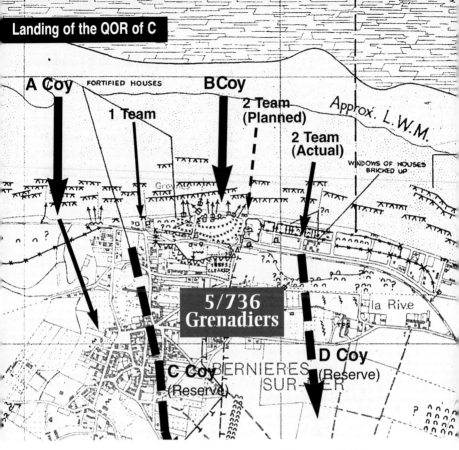

A Coy   FORTIFIED HOUSES   B Coy

1 Team

2 Team
(Planned)

2 Team
(Actual)

Approx. L.W.M.

WINDOWS OF HOUSES
BRICKED UP

5/736
Grenadiers

la Rive

C Coy   BERNIERES   D Coy
(Reserve)   SUR-MER   (Reserve)

'... the LCT grounded on the shore, a sailor in the bows sounded the depth and the ramp went down.

'When the first Flail went out, the lightened craft surged forward a few feet. The second Flail followed and again it surged forward but there was a crump' and the craft lurched as the ramp struck a mine on a submerged beach obstacle. Now it's my turn.

'"Driver Advance!" I order and as we pass over the ramp, a damaged hinge breaks and we lurch, my tank's rotor jib striking another tetrahedra and exploding a shell attached to it. But we are moving onto the wide sandy beach where Jock Stirling and the second flail are already beating up to the wall. I can see the Bridge AVRE moving through the beach obstacles behind them, when there is an explosion on the turret and the bridge falls uselessly. The AVRE tries petarding the sea wall for some time but without success.'

All this took precious time. The infantry of A and B Companies of the Queen's Own Rifles of Canada (QOR of C), who had started landing between 0805 and 0815 hours and were now in cover amongst the beach obstacles and behind the knocked out 'funnies'. The tide was still rising

63

and the Anglo-Canadian landing force needed to get off the narrowing stretch of beach. Battering an eighteenth century style breach in the sea wall would take too long, so as Lieutenant Hammerton, continued:

'That meant Plan Two, so I move up to the foot of a concrete ramp leading to the top of the wall and blow my Cordtex [to clear the turret ring of waterproofing]. Paddy Addis, my gunner clears the barrel and I sight through it just as we did at Orford, and we fire high explosive at one corner of a railway-steel gate called 'Element C' which is blocking the top of the ramp. I carry on aiming and firing until Element C is a wreck. We then back off to let another AVRE climb the ramp to push the wrecked gate away, but the AVRE tips over on its side, one track off the ramp. Another AVRE goes up the narrow ramp and pushes the wreckage to one side – and sets off a mine, which halts it on top of the wall.

'I move up to the foot of the ramp, dismount to attach the towrope to the wreckage which we drag backwards to the sea out of the way. The tide is coming in fast now... I signal to Jock and the second Flail to go up the ramp to start flailing inland. It takes a few minutes to line up on the ramp the foot of which is already under water, but they are up. Just as we are about to follow, my driver says; 'Sir, the water's coming in up to my knees'. Then the engine dies, we are flooded because of having cleared the turret ring. "Bale out!" I yell.'

A route off the beach had been established to the east of WN 28 at the cost of four armoured vehicles.

QOR of C, as already recorded, lost several LCAs on the run-in and, in addition, the tide had set them east by about 200 yards. Consequently, B Company landed directly in front of WN 28 'and immediately caught a packet'. The company group was pinned down on the beach and 'Within the first few minutes there were sixty-five casualties'. Initial attempts to break into the *Wiederstandneste* failed. Ross Munro reported that the

A drowned DD. Canadian and Beach Group Workshops repaired over a hundred drowned vehicles recovered from Juno Beach.

impasse was broken when:

> '... the Toronto troops somehow reached the sea-wall which extends along the back of the beach at Bernières, got over it, and worked their way through the dunes towards the casemate. Meanwhile, some of their troops, including Bren gunners, got into the buildings near the casemate and gave covering fire.'

According to the battalion's war diary, under the covering fire described above, a small, determined attack with grenades and Stens broke into the enemy position and dealt with a pill box that was holding them up:

> 'Lt Herbert, Cpl Tessier and Riflemen Chicoski do a damm fine job in outflanking the enemy position and finally the remnants of the enemy surrender'.

Ross Munro continued:

> 'The Queen's Own then captured one line of trenches after another...' and they were through the vaunted Atlantic Wall but B Company was badly written down and had lost its company commander, its sergeant major, two officers and two senior NCOs. Consequently, junior NCOs such as 'Corporals Red Suddes and Scott carry on with the job of clearing up around the beach exit although many of them are wounded to some extent'.

Meanwhile, A Company QOR of C, landing amongst the dunes to the west of Bernières, was quickly off the beach but having reached the railway line, the company was hit by heavy mortar fire. Pinned down for some time, they suffered significant casualties before they managed to move inland.

Ross Munro

While the QOR of C was fighting through the Bernières strong points, the 79th Armoured Division's assault armour was still, as described earlier,

German command post shelter for WN 28.

establishing their gaps off the beach. A Canadian diarist commented that:

> 'By now the DD tanks and AVREs are on the beach but don't seem to be getting any place. The support all around has been very disappointing as far as we are concerned, for none of the beach defences have been touched and this has caused very high casualties amongst the assaulting companies.'

The disruption of the landing programme gives this complaint some justification but the Canadian Official History concludes 'that the effect of the drenching fire was moral rather than material ... and its effect on the morale of the defenders considerably eased the task of the assaulting infantry'. Colonel Stacey goes on to say, 'that a degree of neutralization was achieved, as there were several instances of weapons which had ample ammunition had not been fired'. Analysis of the generally more accurate artillery battle logs and the ships' logs of the landing craft flotillas indicates that, in most cases, the funnies landed just ahead of the infantry but not necessarily in the same places. However, the important fact is that at this stage, the two arms were *per force* fighting their own battle, not a concentrated combined arms battle, as was planned. The Fort Garry Horse concede this point in their war diary. Nonetheless, support improved when the Shermans of B Squadron joined the QOR of C in fighting towards Objective Yew.

The QOR of C's second wave approached the beach at 0830 hours. The battalion's war diary recorded that:

> 'C and D Coys and Alternate Battalion HQ touch down. The casualties amongst the LCAs are quite heavy, with almost half of them being blown up by under water mines [fixed to the now submerged obstacles]. However, the personnel get ashore without too much trouble and pass through the assault coys' on their way to their positions.'

The phrase 'without too much trouble', would be disputed by some QOR soldiers of D Company:

> 'All our assault engineers were killed in action. We were still in the water when a section was cut down ... The sea was red. One lad was hit in the smoke bomb he was carrying. Another a human torch had the presence of mind to head back into the water. Our flame thrower man was hit and exploded...'

The next entry timed 0900 hours indicates that German resistance was mainly in the 'crust' of defences, rather than in the town of Bernières:

> 'Battalion HQ arrives on shore, linked up with Alt Bn HQ and proceed through the town where a temporary HQ is set up at MR 992848. Alt B HQ detach themselves and set up in a house at MR 994854 where they earn all rights to the house by putting out a fire and gaining the everlasting thanks of the owner. At this time it is noticed that a café just a hundred yards off the beach is opened and selling wine to all and sundry!'

ANTI TANK DITCH

WN28

GAP N1

B Coy
QORC

B Coy
QORC

GAP N2

The assault on Bernières-sur-mer: Nan White.

The D Day house

GAP N1

The Bernières railway station on the edge of WN28, then and now. The building shows signs of Petard damage and the anti-tank ditch has been partly filled.

However, by 0940 the battalion's diarist was reporting considerable confusion as the battalion attempted to regroup. As already noted, B Company was severely written down and was reorganizing into little more than a platoon sized group, while A Company had to extricate themselves from an exposed position west of the town.

St Aubin – Nan Red Sector

On 8 Cdn Brigade's left, the North Shore (New Brunswick) Regiment was the second battalion of the leading assault wave. They had suffered the same problems of delay as the QOR of C, during the run-in to Nan Red. However, as recorded in the N Shore R's war diary, A Company landed at 0810 hours on the battalion's right flank. The battalion's historian recorded that their task:

'... was to clear the beaches, swing right, capture the gap and buildings

68

to the west. On landing the company immediately came under machine gun and mortar fire accompanied by 88mm air burst and in clearing their position of the beachhead sustained fairly heavy casualties from mines and booby traps, but obtained their objective on time and joined up with the Queen's Own Rifles on the right. Lieutenant Keith led his men across the beach to the seawall but a mine exploded killing Sgt Hugh McCormick, L/Sgt Pal Walsh and Cpl Albert Savoy. So Lt Keith rose to his feet and had Pte Elles fetch a Bangalore to blast a lane though the wire. The explosion set off a hidden mine and Lt Keith was terribly wounded while Pte Elles was killed. However, the others got though the gap created by the explosion and house-to-house fighting began.'

A Company reached the line of objective Yew at 0948 hours and their casualties numbered some twenty-five all ranks.

If A Company is regarded as having a hard but relatively straightforward fight, the North Shore's B Company, landing on the battalion's left, faced far sterner opposition at WN 27, on the western edge of St Aubin. The company's briefing had factually described the defences but had painted what proved to be an optimistic picture of the 'German' defenders:

'The strong point was at the highest point of land, and intelligence reports stated it had an estimated garrison of forty all ranks, consisting mainly of low category men evacuated from the Russian front with some Russians and Poles. They are classified as poor troops with morale only fair.'

The battalion's historian outlined B Company's plan for capturing WN 27, which was based on the assumption that the New Brunswickers would have been preceded ashore by both the DDs and the assault armour:

'After reaching the beach, B Company was to reorganize and move immediately to south of the strong point via the beach exit and main lateral road to take up a position preparatory to assaulting the strong point from the rear. Number 4 Platoon would be to the right and Number 5 Platoon to the left for the attack. Number 6 platoon would contain the enemy from the beach until the assault was ready.'

Number 4 Platoon's commander was Lieutenant Richardson who described the run-in to the beach and the devil may care attitude of his soldiers:

'Tracer bullets from a German 20mm anti-aircraft gun seemed to fill the air as we came in but everyone in our boat seemed to take it as just another scheme. In fact the morale was never higher and the platoon was merrily singing 'Roll Me Over, Lay Me Down' as we approached the shore. The Germans held fire until we were fairly close in. Our first casualty was when an armour-piercing bullet came through the LCA and struck Private White a stunning blow in the forehead.'

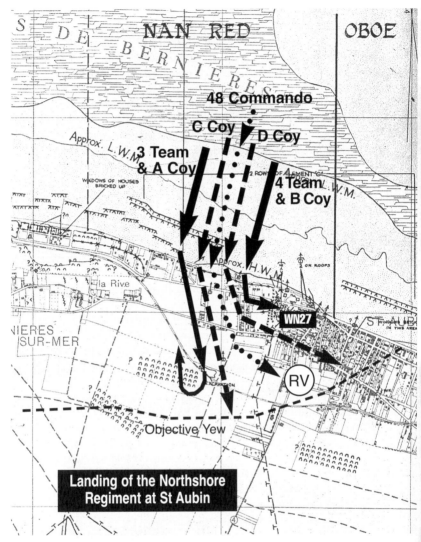

Landing of the Northshore Regiment at St Aubin

Assault armour and beach obstacles photographed from a landing craft during the run-in to Nan Red.

A sequence taken from the film covering A Company's landing on Nan Red, between the German strongpoints WN 27 and WN 28.

Once they were out of the boat, 'everyone acted mechanically, heading for the beach and the cover of the beach wall'. 4 Platoon were fortunate and did not suffer a single casualty as they made for the sea wall and its rolls of barbed wire. Captain Bill Harvey, second in command of B Company, advancing across the beach, watched the platoon use their Bangalore torpedo 'Then we saw a low wire entanglement and the lads swung into action. The fuse was set, there was an explosion and as the smoke cleared the men rushed through...' the resulting gap in the wire and across 'what we later discovered was a minefield'. However, the advance on WN27 slowed as 'The men could see the way in which the enemy had arranged his field of fire and had all approaches covered with machine gun fire. Snipers were cleverly located and could move underground from one point to another.' Lieutenant Richardson pointed out that,

> 'attacking them was difficult as the Germans were behind concrete and we were without armoured support. Soon the sniping became the most demoralizing aspect of the day, as we began to lose one man after another'.

B Company's platoons were 'having a difficult time', with some sections in exposed positions and other sections 'lost' in the confusion of battle.

To make matters worse, the defences 'appeared not to have been touched' by the naval, air and amphibious bombardment. However, after-action analysis concluded that the position had been hit but during the

The area just west of St Aubin where A Company North Shore Regiment landed.

A well camouflaged casemate and a villa damaged by the bombardment on Juno Beach.

extended delay between the lifting of the fire plan and the delayed landing of the assault troops, the German defenders had recovered to some extent. The full neutralizing effect of artillery is of short duration and in this case, the delays prevented the Canadian infantry from benefiting from its full effect during their assault on WN 27.

The German crew of a 50mm anti-tank gun were amongst those who recovered quickly. They initially dominated the eastern portion of Nan Red with their anti-tank fire, knocking out one of the first DD tanks ashore and led to the Allied armour landing further to the west. This left B Company pinned down by machine gun fire on the beach with little support.

79th Armoured Division's history gives an account of the first stage of the action against WN 27.

> 'Number 4 Team touched down 150 yards east of the target – one craft in 7 feet of water. A collision occurred between one landing craft and a bridge AVRE, causing the crew of the latter to dismount. They were at once sniped and attacked with grenades; three were killed and one wounded. Flails on touching down turned west and flailed a lane through the same gap in the dunes as used by Number 3 Team.'

The North Shore Regiment's adjutant described in the battalion war diary how, a little later, they were able to make effective use of armoured

Another view of Nan Red and the half submerged beach obstacles.

support:

> *'B Coy called on the tanks to assist in the reduction of the strong point. Later when the AVREs became available, the Petards mounted on them were used to bombard the defences. The cooperation of infantry and tanks was excellent and the strong point was gradually reduced.'*

An *ad hoc* force of Royal Marine Centaur tanks with their 95mm guns, AVRE's with Petard guns and eventually DD tanks all engaged WN 27's pillboxes and machine gun positions . The 79th Division describes how,

While fighting continued in St Aubin, further west a taped gap used by a Royal Marine Centaur as engineers clear mines.

'A pillbox on the cliff fell to Petard fire and houses belching forth streams of mortar bombs and small arms fire were silenced by 75 mm [flail's main armament] and Petards.'

The official historian recorded that the 50mm gun's crew fought on for about forty-five minutes but 'was put out of action by tank fire'. He continued, 'that about 70 empty shell cases around the emplacement, attested the resolution with which its crew had fought it'.

With WN 27 neutralized by the armour, the infantry of the North Shore Regiment assaulted. The battalion's historian wrote:

'Sergeant Major Murray, Lieutenants McCann and Richardson moved in with B Company for the attack on the strong point. The enemy began to fly white flags but as the assault moved in, opened fire again, which caused more casualties. But the boys drove in and the tanks did their stuff. White flags went up again but the North Shore had had enough of that trickery and went in with bombs, cold steel and shooting. They inflicted many times the casualties the enemy had inflicted on them and cleaned out the place.

The AVREs Petard gun fired a 40 lb demolition round nicknamed the 'flying dustbin'.

'Lt McCann was into the stronghold with his men. It took two hours to thoroughly inspect the main gun positions and their underground connections, and no one knew whether or not we had all the enemy. Four officers and Seventy-five other ranks were taken prisoner, and another fifty were killed or wounded.

Major Forbes realized that the strength of the strong point was much greater than had been anticipated. 'He was further puzzled by the fact that men kept appearing as thought the garrison were being supplied from somewhere.' The mystery was solved when tunnels and covered ways were found and cleared.

The North Shore's war diary recorded that,

'At 11.15 hrs, four hours and five minutes after landing the assault area was cleared, thus one of the Atlantic Wall's bastions that had taken four years to build was completely reduced'.

Nonetheless, Lieutenant Colonel Stacey wrote that 'it was not until evening [1800 hours] did the last defenders of WN 27 finally give in' having been winkled out of the concrete casemates. The North Shore Regiment's capture of St Aubin and the clearance of the coastal villages eastwards by 48 Commando, whose objective was to link up with 3rd British Division on Sword Beach, will be continued in Chapter 6.

Meanwhile, in the gap between St Aubin and Bernières, opposition was relatively light. As already recorded, Major Forbes and the North Shore's A

Company had been quickly across the beach and over the sea wall. However, they 'suffered some casualties in booby-trapped houses but in general made good the beachhead objective without great difficulty'. Landing behind the infantry, 79th Armoured Division's history records that their:

'*Number 3 Team had an easier time, one craft was hit and just made the beach, the other two landed east of the planned gap. Crabs flailed up to the 10 feet sea wall and a bridge was successfully, if steeply, laid. Another Crab flailed a lane through the dunes to the lateral and the reserve Crab widened this.*'

The sea sick soldiers of the North Shore's second wave, C and D Companies, circled off the beach as they waited for their turn to touch down. They had,

'*watched A and B Companies land, as well as three or four tanks of the engineer assault crews, but could tell very little about enemy resistance due to smoke and fire from the town but they were also quickly across the beach*'.

D Company moved on to fight in the southern part of St Aubin. At about the same time, Gunner Roland Johnston a driver of an M10 Tank Destroyer landed on Nan Red with 247 Anti-tank Battery attached to the North Shore Regiment. He recounted an unpleasant part of his move off the beach.

'*... as we came in up closer, you could see bodies all over the beaches. When we got to the beach we drove straight off and we had to run right over a lot of casualties to get up the beach. It was a big worry but you had to put it out of your mind, just forget about it. There was only one way up and you got to realize that the tracks cut down so much in the sand that I wondered at one point if we were going to make it.*

'*Our orders were to go straight up the beach as far as you could. The machine gun fire [from St Aubin] was wild, all over the place. A lot of the infantry were still in the water. They were pinned down and they couldn't get in. The infantry took cover behind every tank that went up the beach.*'

The North Shore's Support Company Commander, Captain Gammon, landed behind C and D Companies to the west of St Aubin and recorded that:

'*Lieutenant Colonel Buell asked me for an anti-tank gun to clear out a pillbox. The pillbox was in the middle of a field 100 yards inshore and the Germans must have been quite frantic as they were throwing stick grenades over the top and none of our fellows were within 100 yards of them. One shot from an anti-tank gun finished that pillbox. Later, I made contact with D Company under Major Anderson, who had gone though to the far edge of the village and had captured the station and vicinity, and C Company under Major Daughney, who was occupying a farm commanding the road to Tailleville. By that time we were well in possession of the village and the only fighting going on was Major Forbes's company attacking the strong point. All the time the Germans were mortaring the town.*

Meanwhile, C Company headed inland towards Tailleville. The battle for Tailleville will be continued in Chapter 5 as a part of the advance inland.

7 Canadian Brigade Group – Mike and Nan Green Sectors

7 Cdn Brigade, as already recorded, had a difficult task in assaulting the Atlantic Wall astride the small fishing port of Courseulles-sur-Mer. This area was the strongest point along the Second Army's front that was to be directly attacked from the sea. Mike Beach and Nan Green Sector were dominated by a pair of strong *Wiederstandneste* and flanking casemates that covered the beach with interlocking arcs of fire. These enemy positions had received the special attention of both bombers and naval gunfire. Even so, it was with some dismay that Brigadier Foster received the message that, despite the ten minute delay already announced, the 79th Armoured Division's assault vehicles were going to be late. He could not delay further and had to order his brigade to attack without the planned support of 'Hobbart's Funnies'. In contrast with 8 Cdn Brigade's experience on Nan Red, support for the infantry of 7 Cdn Brigade and suppression of the enemy's defences would, initially, fall entirely on the shoulders of the DD tanks of the 1 Hussars.

Waiting for Force J's landing craft, was one of a pair of Royal Navy miniature submarines that had been in position for some days, ready to accurately guide the assault force to the beaches. By dawn on 6 June 1944, Lieutenant Hudspeth and his crew of *X20* had spent sixty-four out of the previous seventy-six hours, submerged, waiting on the bottom off Juno Beach. *X20* was now surfaced, exactly 9,000 yards from the coastline. Their role was to mark the centre of Canadian's assault area and the intended disembarkation point for the DD tanks. *X20's* radar reflectors and lights shaded so they shone out to sea, acted as confirmation to the ships' navigators who were confronted by a coastline ahead which was, confusingly, littered with church spires. One British LCT captain commented: 'My landmark was a church at Bernières but with all the smoke, I couldn't tell which bloody spire was which!'

The sea around *X20* was rough and under cover of the bombardment, LCTs were preparing to launch the DD tanks. Tank commander Sergeant Leo Gariepy, of B Squadron, 1 Hussars, was in a LCT at the front of Force J1, heading towards Nan Green Sector in support of 7 Cdn Brigade. He recalled:

'... the minesweepers leading us in slowed down and began making a semicircle. The flotilla of LCTs began manoeuvring for launching our DD tanks. This meant it was necessary for them to head into the wind, showing a broadside to the enemy supposedly alert on the coast. It seemed incredible that we had not been seen.

Courseulles

WN28

R WPG R

7 CDN BDE

3 CDN DIV.

REG RIF

MAP SQUARE CO ORDS
951877 991867
944849 984838

NEG Nᵒ 59385

ET
6347
S.E.

'Our LCT was having great difficulty trying to maintain its position for launching. ... Finally the launching officer called us together and said that High Command had vetoed launching in such a rough sea.

'The LCT began manoeuvring again to bring us right into the beaches. We were then approximately 9,000 yards out, and the spirit had gone out of everyone. We were discouraged and disheartened to realize that all our training had been in vain and we would now be dropped on the beaches like 'gravel crushers' [nickname for the infantry]... Suddenly, at 7,000 yards, our squadron commander, Major Duncan, asked us if we would prefer to risk it. Cheers went up, we were all for it and we prepared to launch. The LCT once again took its launching position in the wind, the ramp was lowered and we each, in turn, rolled off. The manoeuvre was difficult owing to the wind and waves. [2 Cdn Armoured Brigade's report states that the distance from the shore was 2,500 rather than 7,000 yards]

'All our five tanks were successfully launched and we ploughed into the water, trying to adopt a pre-determined attack formation. (We couldn't fire our guns in the water, because they were hidden behind the huge canvas screen that kept us afloat.) Standing on the command deck at the back of my turret, trying to steer and navigate, that 7,000 yards to the beach was the longest journey of my life.

'Enemy fire was discernible now. Machine-gun bullets were ripping the water all around me and an occasional mortar shell fell among us. I looked behind to see how the others were faring and noticed that many of the tanks had sunk and the crews were desperately trying to board bright-yellow salvage dinghies.

A drowning DD tank with the crew safe in their life raft.

The X Craft photographed off Juno Beach.

'*A midget submarine* [X20] *appeared just a few yards in front of me. His duty was to lead me to my primary target on the beach a blockhouse sheltering a naval gun. High wind was forcing me to drift and the man in the submarine was trying to wave me back into line. It was impossible; the wind was too strong. The struts which kept the rubberized skirt around the tank were groaning and I had visions of them giving out at any moment.*

'*I called on my crew to bring up fire extinguishers and tools to try and brace the struts. I could hear the pinging of enemy bullets ripping through the canvas and hitting the hull of my tank.*

'*... when we were a few hundred yards from the beach the destroyer started firing salvo after salvo with a deafening roar. As the water became shallower, the submarine stopped, its occupant* [Lieutenant Hudspeth] *stood up and wished me luck with his hands clasped over his mouth.*

'*Of the nineteen tanks we should have launched I could now only see nine* [fourteen B Squadron DDs eventually landed]. *I was a few yards off my target, but not too bad, and at exactly 0745, I touched the sand and drove out of the water.* [Naval logs record the DD beaching times as 0759 on Mike and 0815 on Nan Green] *On the beach, I gave orders to deflate the canvas skirt and what happened next will always remain vivid in my memory. The German machine gunners in the dunes were absolutely stupefied to see a tank emerging from the sea. Some of them ran away, some just stood up in their nests and stared, unable to believe their eyes. We mowed them down like they were corn on the cobs. The element of surprise was a total success.*'

80

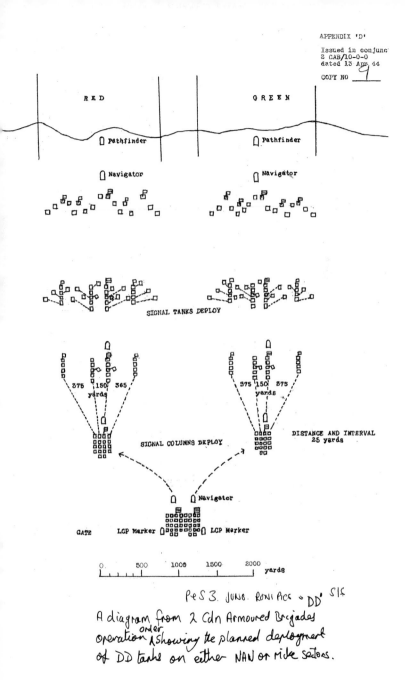

RED   GREEN

⋂ Pathfinder   ⋂ Pathfinder

⋂ Navigator   ⋂ Navigator

SIGNAL TANKS DEPLOY

375   150   365   375 150 375
yards   yards

SIGNAL COLUMNS DEPLOY

DISTANCE AND INTERVAL
25 yards

⋂ ⋂ Navigator

GATE   LCP Marker ⋂░░░⋂ LCP Marker

0.   500   1000   1500   2000
                              yards

PeS 3. JUNO. RONI PICS - DD' SIS

A diagram from 2 Cdn Armoured Brigades
operation order Showing the planned deployment
of DD tanks on either NAN or mike sectors.

Launching and deployment of DD tanks as they swam into the beach. A schematic landing diagram taken from 2 Canadian Armoured Brigade Operations Order.

It would be wrong to assume that the thirty of the thirty-eight Sherman DD tanks that 1 Hussar's leading squadrons had been launched, landed in a coherent wave. Some landed in front of the infantry – B Company of the Reginas issued the code word 'Popcorn' (DD tanks have 'touched down') at 0758 hours and reported their own landing at 0815. Elsewhere, the DDs touched down more or less at the same time as the infantry but on the right. A Squadron's Shermans carried out a deep wade and landed up to six minutes behind the vulnerable khaki clad figures. However, no matter when they landed, the DD tanks were able to provide valuable support to help the infantry cross the beach. Of the approximately sixteen tanks lost to enemy mortar fire or from being swamped, only one crewman was killed. Most of the men successfully used their escape breathing apparatus and were rescued from their yellow life rafts by passing landing craft.

7 Cdn Infantry Brigade planned to land with two battalions leading the assault on the Courseulles area. The Regina Rifles on Nan Green Beach, to the east of the mouth of the River Seulles, were supported by B Squadron 1 Hussars. Landing on Mike Sector, the Royal Winnipeg Rifles, with C Company 1 Canadian Scottish and A Squadron 1 Hussars under command, were to clear Graye-sur-Mer and the area to the west of the river mouth.

The German Defences

6 *Kompanie* 736 Grenadier Regiment held the coastal defences in the Courseulles area. The total of eighty prisoners in addition to those who were killed or escaped indicate that the company was reinforced by at least

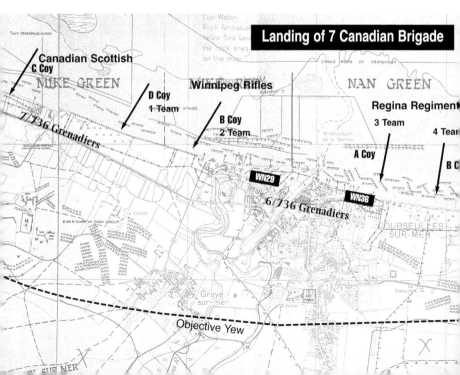

A German coastal infantryman lies dead amongst the dunes.

a platoon. Judging by the photographs and reports that 'some Russians held out in a casemate until 1800 hours', there was at least a platoon of former Soviet troops, probably from 642 *Ost* Battalion attached to 6 *Kompanie*. As already recorded, there were two main strong points in the Courseulles area, astride the mouth of the Seulles River. WN 29 to the east of and WN31 to the west. These two *Wiederstandnests* protected in large M677 concrete casemates, had the only two 88mm guns on 716th Division's entire front between le Hamel and Ouisterham. The guns were mounted to cover the beaches either side of Courseulles. WN 29 was a relatively compact strong point but the houses along the seafront and just inland of the position had been well fortified. Amongst the sand dunes, WN 31 was more extensive, with no fewer than thirteen major concrete structures, and the bend of the River Seulles behind it. Both small bridges into Courseulles were well guarded. Mines and wire were extensively used especially amongst the sand dunes. The town itself while not extensively prepared for defence, did offer the German defenders the opportunity of a fighting withdrawal that could halt or at least slow the Canadian advance inland.

The Regina Rifles – Nan Green

Possibly the most demanding mission had been allocated to the Regina Rifles, who not only had to break through the coastal defences of WN 29 to the east of the river mouth but also to clear the town of Courseulles. The absence of the 79th Division's assault armour, until approximately twelve minutes after they landed, was a serious blow but they did have the DDs of B Squadron 1 Hussars in support. Amongst the first tanks ashore was Sergeant Leo Gariepy:

'Making my way up the long expanse of sand, destroying obstacles as we moved on, I approached the blockhouse that was my target. It was camouflaged with a superstructure to make it look like a beach house, but seeing that the roof had been demolished I assumed it was out of commission and stopped as close to the walls as possible.

'... Several tanks were still wallowing in the water, although many had foundered. Heavy shelling from at sea was still going on, landing craft and infantry assault boats were coming in. It was like a scene out of Dante's Inferno.

'While I was observing all this, our tank was suddenly lifted off the ground by a tremendous blast. I was sure we had copped one, but looking out I saw a huge gun recoiling into the blockhouse by which we were sheltering. It was far from out of action. I realized we were too close for him to get a bead on us and that we were safe for the moment. We withdrew a few yards obliquely from his line of sight and from that position, at almost point-blank range, I ordered several rounds of armour piercing shells to be fired into the embrasure. Then I went round behind the blockhouse and pumped eight or ten high explosive rounds through the steel doors of the entrance.'

Private Heinrich Siebel, attached to 6 *Kompanie* from the 716th Division's *Panzerjagerkompanie* was crewing a 88mm gun in the Courseulles area and might have been amongst Sergeant Gariepy's victims. Siebel wrote:

'... we shot and shot, especially at the strange tanks that came up the beach. It was hard for us to see much because of the smoke but I believe we destroyed two tanks before our gun received a direct hit. There was a flash and a great bang and I was blown backwards onto the concrete floor and knew nothing else for a time. When I woke up I found two of our men dead and more wounded. Our gun was destroyed and all I could think of was escape. I tried to get out through the rear exit, pulling one of my wounded friends with me, but debris made this difficult. There was a lot of shooting, then some British soldiers came and with their help I was able to escape. My comrade was treated, but he died.'

Landing behind the DD tanks, were the leading companies of the Regina

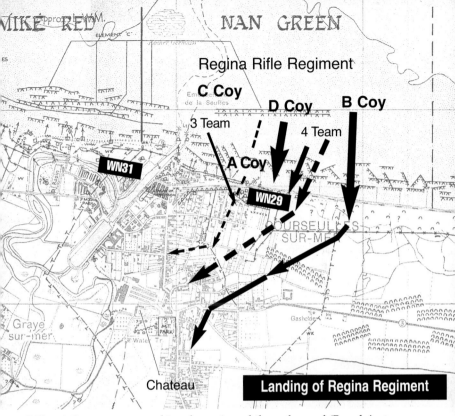

Landing of Regina Regiment

Rifles. A Company, on touching down, issued the code word 'Brandy', at 0809 hours, which was duly recorded in the battalion war diary. At 0815 hours they were joined on the beach by B Company.

Despite the presence of the DD tanks on the beach, the Regina's leading waves were engaged by concentrated machine gun fire from WN 29 and flanking concrete *Tobrukstands*. These positions, held by the infantrymen of 6 *Kompanie*, had survived the air and naval bombardment. According to the Regina's war diarist, the '... pillboxes and other emplacements were still open for business when our troops touched down'. Once again the delay in landing had allowed the defenders time to recover. The report of 505th LCA Flotilla describes A Company's landing on Mike Beach in front of an active enemy:

> 'No. 1 Craft: all troops got clear of the water and then three were seen to fall when running up the beach. No. 2 Craft: Two were hit as soon as they attempted to leave the craft. The remainder of the troops sustained a few casualties when running up the beach. No.3 Craft: Six seen to fall whilst running up the beach. No. 5 craft: A few casualties among the troops once they were clear of the water.'

The Regina's A Company suffered the heaviest casualties, losing about a fifth of their strength in the surf and on the sands in front of WN 29; before they had even started clearing their objective.

B Company, landing six minutes after A Company, waded ashore on the Regina's left flank, to the east of WN29, against lesser opposition, and pushed on over the sea wall and started clearing its designated areas in Courseulles. Meanwhile, A Company was breaking into WN 29 with a left flanking attack supported by the 1st Hussar's DD tanks. They were firing from positions on the beach as the waves and the rapidly rising tide washed around them. The Reginas had the usual heavy concrete casemates and trenches to subdue but also had had to deal with a line of fortified houses, which clustered around the Courseulles railway station. The fighting lasted for over two hours. Once off the beach, and through the mines, wire and into the enemy defences, A Company advanced from trench to trench, efficiently clearing positions with grenade and bayonet. The DD tanks continued to provide close support and fired shells into embrasures of the enemy's casemates, and defended houses until the arrival of 79th Armoured Division's assault teams.

Landing at 0821 hours, the assault armour of Number 3 and 4 Teams belatedly began its tasks of clearing obstacles from the fifty yards of beach that was still yet to be covered by the tide. The two teams played their part in breaching the sea wall for following troops and supported

Anti tank ditch

the Reginas by helping subdue enemy positions that had been impervious to the DD's 75mm gun. However, a Combined Operations operational analysts confirmed that the majority of the enemy positions in the beach area had fallen victim to B Squadron 1 Hussars. The analysist wrote:

> 'The 75 mm gun position at the east end of the strongpoint had fired many rounds (estimated 200 empties) and was put out of action by a direct hit which penetrated the gun shield making a hole 3 inch x 6 inch it is probable that the gun was put out by a direct shot from a DD tank.

> Similarly, the 88-mm. position by the riverside was probably silenced by direct

Sergeant Gariepy's tank in Courseulles on D Day.

> hits with guns from DD tanks, although the concrete and gun shield were marked by shells probably fired by destroyers and LCGs. The nearby 50-mm. gun's shield had been pierced by holes 'probably caused by aimed fire from tank at short range'. Of the strongpoint generally, the guns had fired a considerable quantity of ammunition and were put out of action by accurately placed fire from close range by tanks.'

Sadly, the process of clearing W 29 had to be repeated by A Company. Once the Canadians had moved on into Courseulles, Germans who had either gone to ground in the casemates or had been missed in the maze of trenches or had infiltrated back into the strong point and were again in action. Individual German riflemen made WN 29 an unhealthy place to linger until late in the day.

Meanwhile, the flail tanks and the AVREs, despite their late arrival, speeded progress off on Nan Green for both the assault and following companies. 79th Armoured Division's historian recorded that, having landed too far east, Number Three Team's:

> 'Crabs flailed along to the proposed lane over the dunes and up to the anti-tank ditch where an AVRE laid a fascine. This ramp was then improved by an armoured bulldozer and the lane declared open... 'Number

4 Team, after a similar landing, despatched their Crabs over the dunes to flail a second route to the fascine already placed across the ditch on their gap by the AVRE Squadron Commander. A Second fascine was laid and both gaps improved by DDs: routes to the lateral road [were also] declared open at 0900 hours.'

Unusually, no mines were reported as the minefield was at this point narrow and most of the mines had been set off by the bombardment. Having created the gaps for the following waves to leave the beach, as described in 26 Assault Company's report, the Petard guns played a useful part in reducing or blasting entry points for the Canadian infantry into the defended houses along the Courseulles seafront.

Fighting in Courseulles

During the planning process, the Regina Rifles' Commanding Officer, Lieutenant Colonel Matheson, divided Courseulles into twelve blocks and briefings were so thorough that 'nearly every foot of the town was known long before it was ever entered'. WN 29 was Block One, which as described above, was cleared by A Company, while the remainder of the blocks were divided up amongst the other companies. Ross Munro, filed a report describing the general nature of the fighting:

'With the sea behind them and the Norman fields ahead, they broke through the first line of defences and took on the next string of pillboxes and line of trenches. They went for the fortified houses, blew their way through

German barges in the harbour at Couseulles.

them and worked into the town of Courseulles, fighting up the streets leading from the inlet to the Market Square. By now, the Germans were in confusion, but they stood to fight in small groups at every corner. Off the Market Square was the German headquarters for this coastal sector. It was in a big château with an orchard behind it, in which were located sturdy air raid shelters with steel and concrete roofs and walls. The officers had fled when the fighting Reginas broke into the building. They found a few snipers; wiped them out; cleaned up obvious opposition in the town and passed though to the farmland south of Courseulles.'

An account by Sergeant Leo Gariepy, of B Squadron, 1 Hussars describes the clearance of Courseulles, as the companies moved through the small town, block by block.

'We then started to head into the town of Courseulles. Fearing a mine pattern on the unused street leading away from the beach, I ploughed through the back gardens of the houses. My rendezvous was at the town graveyard, on the Rue Emile Heroult.

'A frantic Frenchman appeared in front of my tank, gesticulating wildly. I stuck my head out of the turret and asked him what he wanted and he shouted 'Boche, Boche' in an excited voice and pointed up the street. When he tried to explain in extremely bad English, I cut him short in French and asked him what was the matter. He was flabbergasted that I could speak French but I finally cooled him long enough for him to tell me that there was a group of enemy hidden inside a large park behind an eight-foot-high wall. A naval shell had made a large hole in the wall and every time the infantry tried to advance past the hole, the enemy sprayed them with machine gun fire.

'An officer in the Regina Rifles

Sand table model being examined in the former German headquarters in Courseulles Château.

asked me if I would block the hole with my tank so his platoon could get by, but not being too fond of being a 'stopper', I suggested that I should go inside the park with my tank and try and dislodge the machine gunners.

'I took a position directly in front of the wall, butted through it with my tank and fired a smoke shell into a large enclosure, following it up with machine-gun fire. Then we fired two HE shells into a sentry box in the far corner of the area. This had the desired effect and some thirty-two German prisoners gave themselves up. I believe this was the first large group of the enemy taken on the beach area.'

Meanwhile, according to his division's history, Major Younger, commander of 26 Assault Squadron had an important task to complete in the town:

'... he personally recced the route into Courseulles, removed the mines and charges from one bridge, swung back another with French assistance, and declared the route from Mike to Nan sectors open at 12.00 hours.'

While the remainder of the Regina Rifles, supported by the DD tanks of B Squadron, were fighting through Courseulles, the final element of the battalion was coming in at 0855 hours. D Company, one of the Regina's reserve companies, had been badly delayed and, with the tide almost fully up on the beach, two of that company's craft struck and detonated mines on now submerged obstacles. Over half the company was lost including the Company Commander, Major Love, who was killed. On reaching the shore the forty-nine survivors nonetheless, assembled and advanced towards the enemy in Reviers as originally planned.

The Royal Winnipeg Rifles – Mike Red

'The Little Black Devil's' mission was to take WN 31 to the west of Courseulles, clear the sand dunes and the sinuous banks of the River Seulles, before pushing forward to Graye-sur-Mer. Major Fulton described WN 31, which was to be attacked by B Company,

'Three large concrete fortifications were their objective. The bunkers were attached to tunnels that ran back behind the sand dunes so they could be easily reinforced'.

Altogether, there were fifteen smaller concrete machine gun positions, along with mortar and anti-aircraft pits, which were connected by a network of trenches. The whole site was surrounded by barbed wire entanglements and mines on the landward side. Major Fulton goes on to record that:

'Just before D Day another cement bunker appeared on the air photos. It was difficult to tell whether it was complete or not and in use, but to make sure, a platoon from C Company was added to B Company's assault. As it turned out the fortification was not completed and the platoon had very little trouble.'

In another change to the battalion's plan the number of assault companies was increased. 'The planners felt that there was too big a gap between 3rd Canadian Division and the 50th Division on our right, so a company from 1 Canadian Scottish Regiment was nominated as assault company to fill the gap.'

In the event, the job of the Winnipegs was made harder by the indifferent results of the bombardment, and the fact that both the DD tanks and the assault armour were to land behind them. This was exactly what the Canadians had planned and trained to avoid. As at Dieppe, unsupported Canadian infantry were destined to attack an alert enemy, secure in concrete positions, dominating the beach.

The battalion started suffering casualties while still some 700 yards from the beach with B Company receiving enemy machine gun and mortar fire. Private Hamilton, whose craft had limped to the beach on a single engine, wrote:

'... we were somewhat separated from our wave, and there was quite a bit of enemy fire on the coast, and we were being heavily fired upon as we approached. I

Two of the larger casemates at WN 31 – casemates then and now.

Mike Green Beach. Photographed in the early afternoon, with vehicles about to move inland.

Graye-sur-Mer

Gold Beach

Gap M1

Destroyed culvert

Courseulles

Gap M2

WN 31

was the second man in our section, and the lad in front of me was Rifleman Gianelli, and as the ramp went down, he took a burst of machine gun fire in his stomach, ahead of me, while I wasn't touched by that burst. There was a tracer in the burst, and you could see it coming to us, and Gianelli was killed instantly.

'I got off the landing craft and crossed the narrow sandy beach to the edge of the beach sand dune. I got some protection, but still, I suffered a piece of shrapnel lodged in my right nostril. I was unconscious for some time...'

Wading ashore in chest high water, the Royal Winnipeg Rifles were attacking with two companies in the first wave. B Company, with two engineer platoons of 6th Field Company, touching down at 0749 hours, landed directly in front of WN 31 and, receiving heavy fire, were forced into the scant cover provided by beach obstacles, shallow shell holes and the sea wall. Teenage grenadier Hans Weiner had held his fire until the Canadians were wading ashore:

'The first Tommies jumped into the sea, which was quite shallow. The bullets hit them and their boats to good effect and I was a little surprised to see them falling – I don't know why. Never having been in a battle before it did shake me to be hurting those men, although they were enemies. Even then in my naivety, I thought that I was only hurting them.

'But we were under fire; bits and pieces were flying all around our embrasures as the Tommies who survived tried to rush behind us. But they seemed to move so slowly as they carried a lot of material, and some more fell. There was so much fire going at them I was surprised to see any survive, and once these reached the upper part of the beach they found some cover and were no longer in our sights.'

On Mike Red, in a manner similar to the US infantry's experience on Omaha, the Winnipegs suffered a steady stream of casualties. Lieutenant Rod Beattie, one of B Company's platoon commanders, was hit in the spine and, unable to pull himself out of the surf, was in danger of drowning. Meanwhile, one of his men, Rifleman Jake Miller, had reached the beach in front of WN 31.

'I was firing into a bunker when a sniper returned fire. Being in the prone position, the sniper's bullet grazed my lower left side. Seconds later a mortar bomb landed on my right side and I got sprayed with shrapnel. A big piece hit my right knee area. I started to crawl forward when Rod Beattie hollered, "Jake don't leave me". I crawled back and tried to pull him away from the incoming tide.'

Lieutenant Beattie was eventually carried to safety by his platoon sergeant.

Ahead, the Winnipegs faced 'four concrete casemates [including the one under construction] and fifteen machine gun positions'. The immediate problem was, however, the belt of wire at the back of the beach. Rifleman,

John McLean, having got across the fireswept beach, recalled that,

> 'The next obstacle was rolls of concertina wire. It was about twenty to thirty feet across this wire and it was about two feet high. Just beyond the wire were the sand dunes and at least temporary safety... However, our Bangalore Torpedo man never made it out of the water so we had to make our way through the wire as best we could.'

McLean was wounded in the legs by splinters from a mortar bomb, while tackling the wire but he regarded himself as lucky, as 'a few feet behind me, one of my comrades was minus his legs and dead'. Some men did get through the wire when,

> 'One of the pioneers section attached to us [B Company] threw himself on the barbed wire so the men could walk over his back and reach the safety of the dunes.'

The 88mm gun covering the mouth at Suelles and the port entrance.

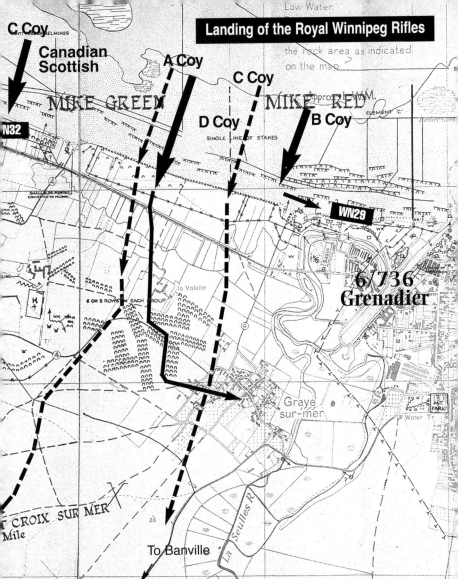

Landing of the Royal Winnipeg Rifles

Despite a few of the leading infantry getting through the enemy's wire, the Winnipegs needed support and looked anxiously out to sea, searching the waves for their supporting tanks and assault armour.

Major Brooks, Commander of A Squadron 1 Hussars, wrote that his DD tanks were launched about 1,500 yards from the beach:

> 'The launching took too long, and the LCTs drifted down [east] on the tide. All craft were not in the proper formation for launching and were being subjected to mortar and other enemy fire.'

The official historian states that one LCT had the chains holding its ramp shot off and another craft, with five tanks aboard off-loaded them directly onto the beach. 'Only ten of A Squadron swam off the LCTs and of these, only seven reached the beach', landing six minutes after the assault infantry companies. The tanks, initially, remained seaward of the obstacles and fired from this position and the squadron commander was told of one enemy group surrendering in their fortifications because of their dismay at seeing tanks already in action.

With belated tank support, as Sergeant Major Belton recorded in B Company's report, 'The sand dunes were reached, and the pill boxes taken by sheer guts and initiative of the individual'. Reporter Ross Munro watched the battle through binoculars and witnessed the bitter infantry fight for WN 31. He recorded that the 'Little Black Devils' fought:

'From dune to dune, along the German trench systems and through the tunnels, these Manitoba troops fought every yard of the way. They broke into the big casemates, ferreted out the gun crews with machine guns, grenades, bayonets and knives. The Canadians ran into crossfire. They were shelled and mortared mercilessly even in the German positions but kept slugging away at the enemy. The 1st Hussar's tanks churned through the dunes in close support and after a struggle which was as bitter and savage as any ... the Winnipegs broke through into the open country behind the beach.'

The fighting, which had been hand to hand had cost B Company ninety casualties. The company's after action report provides a stark insight into the nature of the battle:

'Rifleman Kimmnel, a signaller attached to the Company, showed outstanding courage in silencing one pillbox. Corporal Slatter, after being hit in the stomach, was seen on his hands and knees still trying to get up to the pillbox, at the same time trying to direct his remaining section by shouting orders. It is reported that Corporal Klos was badly wounded in the stomach and legs while leaving the craft but made his way to the enemy position and was found there, apparently having killed two of the Hun and was sitting on one, with his hands still gripped on his throat. ... Captain Gower, without thought of safety for himself, encouraged his men and controlled the situation, in full view of the enemy, bareheaded as he had lost his helmet after an incident in the water. It is the opinion of the remaining few that his courage and amazing coolness, was one of the outstanding factors in our success in pushing through the first objective.'

Grenadier Hans Weiner, inside one of the casemates, describes the latter stage of the battle, after he and his fellow soldiers were surrounded by the Canadians and being engaged by all available weapons.

'Tanks began shooting at us with cannon and machine gun and we were forced to get down. Part of our blockhouse collapsed and we thought we would be buried alive. By some miracle we were not and our Gefreiter

Tobrukstand – concrete position for one machine gun.

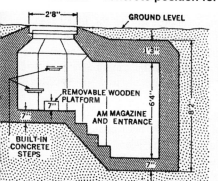

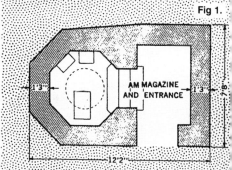

Fig 1.

American intelligence sketches of a *Tobrukstand* – German concrete machine gun post.

A *Tobrukstand* at WN 31. This example is almost certainly for a medium mortar.

reached us to say that all the other men were dead or wounded – but we would not give up. Then some of the Tommies came very close as they fired and we knew it was hopeless. The enemy were shouting and firing and then we ran out of ammunition, so it seemed the sensible thing to surrender, if we could do so without being shot.

'We threw our helmets out of the hole at the back and they called us out. Ten Tommies were all pointing their guns at us. After being searched we were told to go and lie on the beach, which was still under fire. It seemed hours before we were taken down to a landing craft for England.'

At the end of the two hour battle for WN 31 only Captain Gower and twenty-six men were still on their feet. It had been one of D Day's most savage fights. Against all odds, B Company had succeeded despite dangerous delays that allowed the enemy to recover his balance after the fine plan and the lack of armoured support during the initial stages. However, the seventy-five percent casualties suffered by B Company, the Winnipeg Rifle's heroic battle proves that the D Day invasion only succeeded because of the generally effective assault armour and integrated fire plan. Similar casualties spread along the entire front would have been totally unsustainable.

With WN 31 subdued, Number 15 Platoon, who were under command of B Company, 'forced a crossing of the R Seulles [as indicated on the map] and cleared out the four enemy positions on the 'Island'.

When asked who in B Company Group should be recommended for bravery, Sergeant Major Belton replied:

'No individual that he knew of could be recommended more than any other ... and there was not a man who went to ground until he was hit.'

However, Captain Gower, whose 'powerful leadership and courage' in the fighting in WN 31 was recognized and awarded one of the most well deserved Military Crosses ever issued to a Canadian soldier.

A little further to the right, 'D Company met lesser opposition while landing, as it was clear of the actual strong point area'. With the enemy infantry in WN 31 fighting for their lives against an immediate threat, D Company was across the beach, through the shredded barbed wire and into the dunes relatively quickly with few casualties. However, without their flail tanks, a minefield in the pasture beyond the dunes halted them. A platoon of 6th Field Company Royal Canadian Engineers, who should have been clearing the beach, were redirected to assist the infantry by hand breaching the minefield, as their beach obstacles were now under water. D Company were soon on their way to la Valette and Graye-sur-Mer encountering further minefields, 'some of which proved to be dummies, at every turn'. The Germans had marked minefields with the *Achtung Minen* signs stencilled in either yellow or white paint. It was only later in the day that word circulated that the signs in yellow paint were dummy minefields

The WN31 command post casemate survived intact. However, the steel OP cupola was cut off after the war.

and could be ignored.

Coming in approximately twenty minutes after their initial assault wave, the Winnipeg's reserve companies, A and C, were quickly into the sand dunes. However, the Winnipeg's Battalion Headquarters had a hard time getting across the beach.

> '*The Bn Comd Gp, landing at 0820 hrs came under mortar and MG fire and were sniped from the left* [area of WN 31] *but managed to get inland by crawling over bogged AVREs and slithering along a low bank*'.

Just seven out of fifteen men from 'Battalion Main' survived the beach. Alternate Battalion HQ, under the Second in Command and the Adjutant, '...with the No. 22 W/T set as a target, were pinned down for two hours'.

Landing with the Winnipeg's Mortar Platoon some time after 0900 hours, Jim Parks recorded how he landed from an LCT along with an

A posed photo taken inside a German artillery command post.

armoured bulldozer. Contrary to the plan that had him driving his carrier across the secured beach and dunes into a baseplate position, the beach was still under fire at a relatively late stage of the landing.

'Our touch down was delayed because we hit a mine tied to a barrier and it threw the craft slightly off course. Then a 75 mm shell hit the left front of the craft where a sailor was winding down the door. He continued to wind it down despite being seriously wounded. The armour piercing shell came through the ramp, and luckily for us it hit the large bulldozer blade at an angle and ricocheted up and away leaving only a large gouge in the blade. The bulldozers left the craft but we were about 250 yards from shore and Sergeant Tommy Plumb, on orders from the Boat Commander, said lets get going. I took one look at the bulldozer and it had water lapping near the top of the cockpit. That meant it was 12 feet deep and our mortar carriers were waterproofed to travel in water only four feet deep. In any event the carrier drove off and into the water. It seemed to float awhile and started to sink. Some of the crew swam for Compo boxes and hung onto them (all this with the tracers flying about). Stringbean White hung on to his food box until picked up by the Navy later. ... We were next to go and into the deep we went. As we sank we started throwing off our heavy equipment, fortunately we had left our buckles undone and we did not want to be weighed down.

'... an LCA just missed me by a whisker and I swallowed about a quart of water and nearly bought it. About 25 – 30 yards ahead of me the LCA started disembarking and I still couldn't touch bottom with my boots. I was able to scramble in just behind the last section wading in. By the time I reached the shoreline I had passed two or three wounded lying face down and grabbed them by the collar and dragged them to dry ground. That started something. I spent a few frantic moments dragging a few more in. I remember Rod Beattie who moaned and said he was numb. I dragged him further in so he wouldn't drown. All hell had been breaking loose. I had only my vest and helmet. Another platoon had gotten through the embankment further to the left. When I had a chance to look around I could see that quite a few of the gang had been caught in the crossfire, some on the barbed wire, some in the water, and on the shore. L/Cpl. Martin was right beside me and had been mortally wounded. I dragged him to the cover of the pillbox near by and went out to an Armoured Bulldozer and I pointed out that Bales and one or

Rare photo of a Royal Engineer D7 armoured bulldozer clearing the rubble on D Day.

*two others were hanging on to barriers in the water and the driver drove back
out to the barrier In about 6-7 feet of water plus waves and picked them up.'*

The Canadian Scottish

According to their war diary D Day started for the battalion when:

> *''Wakey, Wakey' was heard over the LCI's PA system and the officers,
> NCOs and men of the 1st Bn. Canadian Scottish Regiment arose to face the
> greatest day in their military career. "Now is the time" said one of the lads,
> "when we can tell whether our instructors knew what it was all about".
> There was no fuss, no sign of the "jitters", the troops ate their breakfast and
> then prepared to embark on the LCAs.'*

1 Canadian Scottish were 7 Cdn Brigade's reserve during the
landing phase. However, C Company was under command of
the Winnipeg Rifles and attacked objectives in Mike Green
Sector in the first assault wave. They left their LCAs:

> *'... in about three feet of water, just short of the beach
> obstacles. At first there was no fire but as we moved forward,
> the odd mortar bomb landed amongst us and MG fire started to
> come from our left flank and Pte Ashley was hit with
> shrapnel in the leg. Several others were hit but more or*

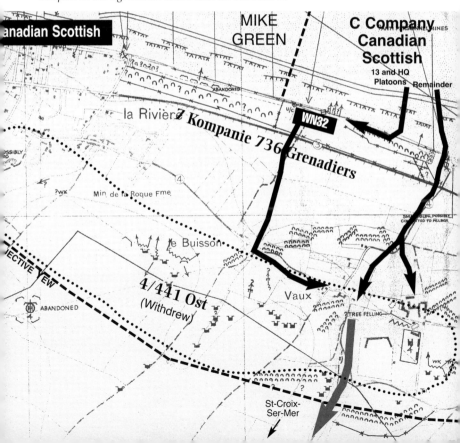

The double anti tank gun casemate on Mike Green had been built in an obvious position and had been well hit by the bombardment.

less unnoticed at the time. Stretcher-bearers started the good job that they were continued to do all day.

'13 Pl and Coy HQ moved west along the beach to their objective only to find – thanks to the Royal Navy – the pillbox was no more. Finding this they moved inland up the road towards the Chateau and cleared out various snipers in the positions further inland. Pl HQ and another section moved to the west and took out an MG and a 105mm gun, which was unmanned. An attempt to turn this prize on the enemy was unsuccessful. It was at this stage that the first two prisoners were taken'

Along Juno Beach, it had taken about two hours to subdue the German defenders of three of the four main *Wiederstandneste* and sundry intermediate positions. The Canadians can claim to have broken one of the strongest parts of Hitler's Atlantic Wall on the invasion coast. However, some Germans still fighting amongst the ruins of their positions sniped at troops attempting to move inland for most of the day. On the eastern flank, WN 27 on the outskirts of St Aubin continued to resist behind Juno Beach. The villages held numerous German troops who would have to be cleared before a viable beachhead could be declared.

WN 28   WN 29   Courseulles

The view from the casemate above looking down Mike and across river to Nan Green Beach.

Chapter 4

The Beachhead

By the time the two assault brigades' reserve battalions arrived on Juno Beach, the tide was nearly fully in and the majority of the German beach obstacles between low and high-water marks were almost covered. The French Canadians of the Chaudiere Regiment and the Canadian Scottish had a difficult landing. Commander Kenneth Edwards in his book *Operation Neptune* recorded:

> 'The Landing Craft Obstacle Clearance Unit did magnificent work, but the speed of the assault was such that they had insufficient time to neutralize or demolish many of the obstacles. ... On the whole, however, the majority of the obstacles were cleared by the simple method of the larger and heavier types of landing craft charging the beaches and crashing their way through the obstacles. At the same time the smaller types of landing craft threaded their way in between the obstacles.'

This method of 'charging through the obstacles with the heavier types of landing craft led to damage and to casualties'. However, to delay would mean reducing the momentum of the assault and there was no other option available to the Royal Navy and Royal Marine landing craft crews. A

Reserve battalions landing on Nan Green, even though the beach was still under intermittent fire.

Canadian Naval report describes the trouble caused by the mined beach obstructions:

'HMCS Prince David *landed her first body of invasion troops exactly on schedule on the beach at Bernières-sur-Mer. The soldiers, members of a French-Canadian* [Chaudiere] *regiment ... were ferried from the parent ship by the landing craft flotillas... It was not until the assault infantry and tank landing craft were practically on the beach that they ran into trouble in the form of mines. The small assault boats were the heaviest sufferers. ... Their way lay through a section of hedgehogs and posts, which gave this piece of water the appearance of a field filled with stumps. These were the mine supports. First Lieutenant J. McBeath's boat was mined; then Lieutenant Buckingham, Lieutenant Beveridge and Leading Seaman Lavergne had their craft smashed by mines. It was a wild scramble for shore, but every one made it with the exception of two French-Canadians... They were killed outright by the mine which their boat hit. ... Chunks of debris rose a hundred feet in the air and troops, now hugging the shelter of a breakwater, were peppered with pieces of wood. The bigger landing craft did not escape, but they could take it.'*

Aboard this second wave of larger craft was Lance Corporal Stuart Stear, a Royal Engineer serving with 103 Beach Group. He explains that his company had eventually landed, having spent some considerable time going around in circles, behind the 'Chauds'.

'We were due to land about 11 o'clock and, as we went in, we passed HMS Ramillies [almost certainly HMS *Belfast] and HMS* Diadem *who fired over us and all the other ships each with a barrage balloon. The noise was tremendous and as we got closer, we could see explosions on the back of the beach or just inland. Only twenty years old and in my first battle, I was scared stiff.*

'On the run in, I saw an infantry landing craft blow up on a mined beach obstacle. It seemed to leap up out of the water and it fell back in several pieces. Other boats had their hulls ripped open by Belgian Gate obstacles but our landing was almost dry. Clutching my toolbox, I rode ashore in our Company workshop truck, passing a lot of bodies, mostly Canadians, washing back and forth in the surf.'

In front of Lance Corporal Stear were the infantry companies of the Chaudiere Regiment, who impressed him with the business like way they were quickly across the beach and heading inland.

'The beach, Nan Red, just west of St Aubin, was under occasional bursts of long range machine gun fire from the direction of Langrune-sur-Mer and from sporadic artillery or mortar fire. The machine gun fire was eventually stopped about midday when about five landing craft came in and

A knocked out Bren gun carrier belonging to the QOR of C and a drowned truck on Nan Beach.

took it in turn to fire their rockets at what was I suppose a strong point. I heard about one of our Sergeants being told to take on a pill box. Apparently he replied, "I'm an engineer not an infantryman." But having been told that he was "A soldier first" he set off with six Sappers to do the job but by the time he got to the pillbox, the infantry had already captured it.

'We hurried across the beach to the cover of the seawall. I only saw one knocked out tank on the beach but there were plenty of vehicles. I read that Montgomery had complained that there seemed to be more vehicles on the beach than troops! We waited here for our recce party to return from checking out the water tower just inland from St Aubin that we were to fix to provide a water supply. At this point, I ate some of the chocolate and boiled sweets from our new and unfamiliar 24 hour ration packs. I can't remember when I got round to eating my hard biscuits and using the Oxo cube sized tea ration – complete with dried milk and sugar.

'It seemed to be absolutely chaotic on the beach at this time but I suppose there was order, as the infantry from our LCT and others gathered by the sea wall and were setting off inland very quickly. The Royal Navy Beach Master was able to call in the landing craft when there was space.'

While the reserve infantry battalions of 7 and 8 Cdn Brigades were quickly across the beach, the armour, self-propelled guns and numerous other vehicles needed a 'gap' to get off the beach. However, by mid-morning, traffic jams of vehicles were beginning to form on the beaches as they

Bernières Station　　　　**Gap N1**

LCIL 299

The Stormont, Glengarry and Dundas Highlanders wade ashore from their LCIs in the Bernières aera on Nan White.

The original small box girder bridge laid by an AVRE as one of the first routing off the beach has been complimented by a bulldozed second ramp.

26

BEACH CO

queued to make their way through the tenuous gaps or in some cases, yet to be opened gaps, into the area behind the dunes or into the coastal villages. Fortunately, the tide was now falling or there would have been even more drowned vehicles blocking the beaches. Despite the delayed landings by the infantry, armour and 79th Armoured Division's special breaching equipment along with the defenders recovery from the shock of the bombardment, 26 and 80 Assault Squadrons and the Canadian field engineers were soon busy producing the tracked and wheeled vehicle gaps off the beach. The initial gaps were not necessarily where planned, due to the continuing resistance by some of the German *wiederstandneste*.

Rudimentary gaps were reported as being open on Nan White Sector as early as 0850 hours. Here the ramp off the beach forced by Lieutenant Hammerton's 75mm gun was open and soon supplemented by an AVRE laid Small Box Girder Bridges (SBGs), which provided routes over the ten foot high sea wall. The brigade battle log noted that as 'Obstructions are being cleared on Nan Green, heavy fire reported beyond the beach. Mike Red – Small arms fire only now.' However, the official historian recorded that:

> 'By 1040 hours, two exits had been opened on Nan Red and three on Nan White, a decidedly more favourable situation than that obtaining on the beaches to the west, where flooded ground proved a serious hindrance.'

As will be seen below and in Chapter 6, Nan Red remained under fire and its gaps were not fully used until late in the day.

The M2 Gap

On Mike Beach, the engineers of 26 Assault Squadron's Number 1 and 2 Teams, landing west of Courseulles, had to contend with some difficult sand dunes and a flooded area beyond, before armour could fan out to support the advance inland. The Brigade Intelligence Summary described the task: 'A sandy road 8 to 10 ft wide runs inland 360 yards to a tarmac lateral road. Ramping of dunes, widening and surfacing is required to

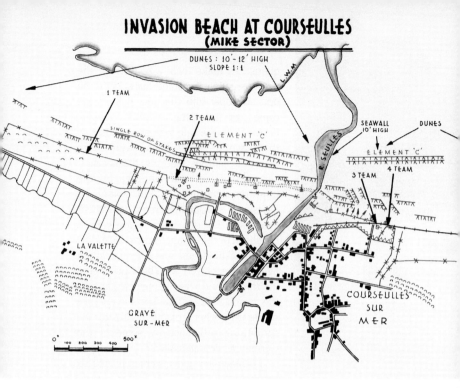

79 Armd plan of Mike sector.

make exit.'

Sergeant Fielder was commander of one of the AVREs heading for the beach to the west of WN 31 where, it will be recalled, B Company, the Winnipeg Rifles were fighting:

'You could see fire going every way. Our people were still shelling and there was still bombing going on. As we were going in we were fired at from a pillbox, but then one of the gun tanks on another craft fired at it and hit the aperture and they weren't able to fire again, so we were lucky there.

'We were slightly late landing. The Canadian infantry had gone in before us and were lying all over the beach and in the water. We thought at first they were Germans, but they weren't and we ran over some of them because we didn't realize who they were. It was only later we found out they were Canadians. We felt terrible, absolutely terrible, because we didn't even know if they were already dead or not.'

Other harrowing accounts, from both British and Canadian drivers, describe the necessity of driving over Canadian infantry, lying wounded on the beach and in the dunes.

Despite the haunting trauma of the beach, on their D Day début, the AVREs and Crabs proved to be technically capable of dealing with the dunes but beyond the sand, 26 Assault Squadron's difficulties really began.

The 79th's divisional historian recorded that:

> '... both teams were put down just opposite No.2 Team's gap [M2]. Two Crabs cleared a lane up to and over the sand dunes, then both broke tracks, striking mines while turning. A third Crab passed and managed to flail a single track clear of the beach and 150 yards inland, as far as a flooded crater sixteen feet wide and twelve feet deep caused by a demolished culvert. Its gun remained in action [but in attempting to by-pass the obstacle] the tank was well and truly bogged. The tank commander Lieutenant Barraclough ... later from his watery resting-place, shattered the Graye-sur-Mer church tower – an observation post.'

See aerial photo on page 92

This crater blocking the road across the flooded area beyond Gap M2, was almost certainly not caused by a deliberate German demolition of the culvert. It was probably hit by one of a stick of bombs dropped by the Allied airforces during their part in subduing the beach defences.

The immediate response by squadron commander, Major Younger, was to redeploy most of the remaining 'funnies' 600 yards further west on Mike Green. The M1 gap was open by 0930 hours, allowing armour off the beach to follow the infantry inland. Meanwhile, at M2, another AVRE had been summoned up by engineer troop commander, Captain Hewitt, to drop its fascine in the hole. The AVRE, named *Charlie One*, approached the flooded pit and promptly slid into it. Under fire and unable to recce the task Captain Hewitt had not been able to see that the job was beyond the capabilities of fascines to solve. But with an AVRE now filling the pit, the Royal Engineer's ability to improvise a solution came to the fore. Captain Hewitt and his Sappers dropped a fascine into the landward side of the pit. Then Number 1 Troop's SGB was laid onto the almost submerged tank's turret. However, the route was still not viable for armour and all

Charlie One, recovered, painted and presented on a plinth.

Gap M2

WN31

available men were summoned to carry logs that the Germans had dumped behind the beach for use as beach obstacles. With the logs dropped into the crater a precarious route was soon in use. Major Younger recorded that,

> '...at about 0915 hours, the first DD tank got across behind the assaulting [infantry] companies. Six tanks got across before the tank bridge started to slide off the turret of the sunken AVRE'.

This troop of Shermans was able to provide valuable support to the infantry, who were pushing inland towards objective Elm. Work continued throughout the morning to keep M2 open and trickle vital armoured support off the beach. Repeated boggings of vehicles on both banks of the pit ensured that the M2 gap continued to be of marginal value until late morning, when rubble and sand was brought up to fill the pit and the route became, as planned, one of the two routes off Mike Red.

Further east, Sergeant Fielder was aboard one of the AVREs making its way inland to an objective at the edge of WN 29:

> 'We were supposed to go up over the dunes to where they thought, from aerial photographs, that there was a ditch. But as luck would have it, when we got up there, there was no ditch. Then we started getting fired on by some Jerries in a dugout. We fired back at them with our Browning and they came out, about five of them, with their hands up. They were only youngsters. We sent them back to the beach, where there was a pen for prisoners. We shed our fascines and went on a little, but then I decided myself that we could do more by going back to the beach.'

Just over two hours after the initial landings, orange windsocks, coloured smoke and a variety of coloured signs, at eight points along Juno Beach indicated that routes for infantry, tanks and wheeled vehicles were open. Hitler's Atlantic Wall had been comprehensively, if not yet completely breached.

The Landing of 9 Cdn Brigade

The 3rd Canadian Division's reserve brigade had the unenviable task of waiting in their small landing craft off shore for the order to land. They spent,

> '...hours going around in circles, glimpsing the smoke and flashes of the battle going on along the beaches. In the rough sea off the beaches, seasickness was rife, as we marked time before landing. It was thoroughly miserable. We couldn't wait to be ashore.'

Major General Keller had two options for 9 Cdn Brigade and had prepared plans to land either on Nan, behind 8 Cdn Brigade (Plan A) or behind 7 Cdn Brigade on Mike Beach (Plan B) to the west of Courseulles. General Keller would select which option to take, having monitored progress from his headquarters aboard HMS *Hilary*. It was clear from radio reports and

9 Canadian Brigade landing. Note the bicycles that were supposed to be used to speed their advance inland.

the easily visible traffic jam on Mike Beach that Plan A, to land 9 Cdn Brigade on Nan Beach, was the obvious option. At 1015 hours, Brigadier Cunningham, aboard his headquarter ship *Royal Ulsterman*, received the code word 'Katnip now'. However, due to the fighting at WN 27 they could not use Nan Red and they were forced to land in a succession of waves on Nan White. The official historian wrote, 'Offshore obstacles were still in position and landings were made even more difficult by the presence of so many wrecked landing craft'.

However, at 1140 hours, the brigade's landing ships touched down but in some cases, the rifle companies could not be immediately disembarked because of congestion on the beach and its exits.

Despite some delays, 9 Cdn Brigade were across the beach with very few casualties and the entire brigade, including its armoured regiment were crammed into Bernières, which was still occupied by the Chaudiere Regiment. As noted by the brigade war diarist, '... there was a bad traffic jam in the town, which took some time to untangle', stretching as it did back onto the beaches. This created yet more delays on the single route that 9 Cdn Brigade could use to reach their assembly area just south of the

Tanks of the Sherbrook Fusiliers come ashore at midday.

town. Here the brigade formed up and waited for almost two hours until 8 Cdn Brigade moved on inland. As will be seen in the next chapter, an enemy position at Talleville, complete with anti-tank guns, had halted the Canadian advance.

Major General Keller had ordered 9 Brigade to land on Nan White, having based his decision on the perfectly sound information available to him at the time, before the problem at Talleville became apparent. However, even if 9 Cdn Brigade had been directed to land on Mike Sector, it is likely that the one good gap (M1) and the one poor gap (M2), along with the marshy ground behind the beach would have led to similar results.

One effect of the traffic jam was that the Canadian self-propelled artillery regiments, who had earlier been firing in their amphibious role, could not motor across the beach and drive inland to their first designated gun positions. Consequently, they found themselves firing their first 'dry land' engagements, on the beach with the waves lapping around them.

Clearance of the Beach

With the strong points either taken or largely subdued, clearing the beach and its immediate hinterland of obstacles and mines was the next priority. This was to be followed by firmly establishing the control organization and the beginnings of the logistic infrastructure that were as vital to OVERLORD's success, as the assault itself. Landing with the first assault troops were the Royal Navy and Combined Operations Beach Masters, along with movement control detachments and their signals sections. Their role was to call in landing craft as combat and logistic priorities and space on the beach dictated. In short they formed the first link in the chain that kept the forward units supplied. From the outset the demand for combat supplies, ammunition, fuel and food, was equalled by the demand for replacement men and vehicles and spares. All these resources had to be brought ashore in increasing volume, in parallel with the need to build up the number of combat troops that were needed ashore to fight the battle. The Allied landings across the beaches had to exceed the German's ability to reinforce the Seventh Army by road and rail.

Canadian Captain Clarke, of Number 1 Movement Control Unit, was amongst the first logistic troops to arrive on Juno. He described his landing with the infantry:

'Those last few moments were pretty awful. We were coming under intense small-arms fire and everyone was down as much as possible. I manoeuvred into a position to be as near as possible to the front. I wanted to be one of the first to land, not because of any heroics but because waiting your turn on the exposed ramp was much worse than going in.

'A sergeant and a corporal started down. I was third. The sergeant couldn't touch bottom but pushed away and swam in towards shore. The corporal started to follow and I plunged in after him but the weight of my 'light assault jacket', filled with enough canned goods to start a grocery store, pulled me under ... I got back onto the ramp and the skipper of the LCI very sensibly decided to pull off and try to come in a bit better.

'The next run at the shore put us in about five feet of water. A naval fellow in a lifebelt went in with a rope and I followed. ... Some of the men had great difficulty getting ashore, particularly the short ones. One poor chap was crushed to death when the ramp broke away in the heavy seas and slammed him between it and the side of the ship. Many of the lads on our LCI never got ashore: a Spandau *opened up just when the water was full of men struggling to get ashore.*

'The beach was littered with those who had been a jump ahead of us and a captured blockhouse being used as a dressing station was literally surrounded by piles of bodies.

'I didn't lose much time getting to the back of the beach where there was a bit of protection and wriggled out of my assault jacket which I swore then and there never to wear again.'

Once ashore, amidst the chaos of battle, numerous essential tasks had to be started immediately if the battle to build up and sustain force levels was to be won. For example, military policeman, Corporal Long had to marshal and control the tracked and wheeled vehicles making their way through N1. He remarked that:

'It wasn't at all like the exercises we had done at Hailing [sic] Island [FABIUS]. *It was all confusion and we were under occasional fire most of the morning and into the afternoon but we got on with our tasks.'*

The RMP had to establish a traffic control system that made the most effective use of the gaps and ensure that priority vehicles were clear of the beach as soon as possible and heading towards their designated assembly areas.

Lance Corporal Stuart Stear and his fellow Sappers of 619 Independent Field Park Company RE had been tasked to repair the water tower at Bernières, which was to be the first water point established by 103 Beach Group.

> 'When the recce party returned they told us that the water tower was undamaged despite the bombardment and destruction around it. So being spare, we were sent to the gaps or lanes off the beach to help clear mines. I remember a tank breaking down in the lane and the officer commander being told by a Royal Navy officer that he had five minutes to get it going or we'd blow his tank up. We had these heavy packed charges about two foot six square that we would put in the hull of a broken down tank to completely demolish it and clear the lane. In this case, the tank was moved but one packed charge had to be used to clear a tank on another lane.

> 'Behind the seawall, the German defences seemed to be freshly built and the ground floors of the houses had been filled with concrete to make camouflaged bunkers. They had been badly shelled and were badly pitted but it was mainly superficial damage. Lying all about were khaki and field grey bodies. More field grey than khaki but it didn't mean anything to me, as I was numb and overwhelmed by all that was going on. Beyond the sea front, there was less damage than I had expected.'

Sergeant Fielder, an AVRE commander of 26 Assault Squadron RE, recalled that, with the infantry moving inland with the support of the Shermans of

An RMP NCO watches the armour and equipment coming off the beach near to D Day House at Bernières.

1st Hussars and the Fort Garry Horse, he was ordered to return to Mike Beach.

> *'So we went back and started clearing the beach of tetrahedrons, connecting them onto a couple of towropes and pulling them clear. In a matter of hours, we'd cleared the beach completely. We were still under fire, but more and more troops were coming in, thick and fast.'*

Lance Corporal Stear spent most of the day working on the 'chaotic' Nan Beach and the area immediately behind the sea wall, clearing obstacles and mines:

> *'Most of the mines were Teller anti-tank mines, which were not too dangerous to handle as they were designed to be set of by vehicles not men. We did find some S or jumping mines in a field beyond the village that were much more sensitive and difficult to clear. One of the men who had been in boy's [apprentice] service with me, Sapper Spreadbury, was killed while he was trying to deal with a booby trapped mine in the dunes behind the beach. There wasn't even enough left of him to fill a sandbag. Despite incidents like this, people quickly became blasé about clearing mines and needed to be swapped around quite frequently. Men lifting mines for the first time were the most thorough. While we were lifting mines by hand, the flail tanks cleared areas behind the dunes for the dumping of stores and the assembly of fresh troops.*

'Another task we began on D Day and continued for several days, was the clearance of obstacles from the beach at low water, as all the stores, men and ammunition had to be landed there. My job was to fit an armoured bulldozer's chains to the obstacles so they could be dragged into piles at the back of the beach.

'During the afternoon, I saw German prisoners passing us being marched back to the beach. They seemed very young and as frightened as we were. Later, others came back on their own, unescorted, happy to be on their way to England and out of the war. The German prisoners helped with carrying stretchers on to the empty landing craft and were put to work burying their dead.

'By late afternoon, the seeming chaos of the morning had been replaced by order, with signs and military police everywhere and by early evening even the sporadic artillery fire had stopped.

Meanwhile, just inland from the beach Germans were being flushed out of their hiding places. Captain 'Nobby' Clarke was again an active participant:

'The afternoon and evening was devoted to "de-lousing" the houses behind the beach of snipers and quite a job it was. We were a bit clumsy at first and lost quite a few because of it, but it soon became more or less a drill. I had a small group of two sergeants and six Sappers with plenty of guts. Some of the houses just refused to be de-loused and so we burnt them down. We set one on fire which had caused us a lot of grief and when it really started to brew a young Jerry made an effort to escape through a window. He got partly out when a gunner on an LCT saw him and hit him with a streak of about fifty Oerlikon rounds.'

An essential part of bringing order to the beachhead was the grim task of collecting the dead. Nothing would have undermined the morale of troops coming across the beach and heading for the front as the sight of mangled bodies. Captain Hall, was the beach master for the Regina Rifles on Mike Red Beach and described how after his battalion had moved inland, he:

'... just hung around the beach. There was lots to see, people to help. We started to collect casualties. German prisoners of war started to come on to

Hedgehogs and Belgian gates (Element C) piled at the beach of Juno within days of the landing.

German prisoners gathered on the railway station platform at Bernières. Note the tree trunks and rails for beach obstacles.

the beach in fair numbers. ...later in the day, when the tide went out, we saw a lot of the casualties that had been drowned, so I got a party of prisoners to start picking up bodies, including the body of the company commander who had followed me in but didn't make it.

'We brought them in and part of my job was also gathering the effects of those killed in action, turning money over to the paymaster and anything

German PWs assembled in the shelter of the sea wall at WN 28 along with wounded. The men guarding them are from 103 Beach Group.

else belonging to them to the Padre. I made notes on how they were killed –
shell wound, drowning and so on.'

Not only was it essential to build up logistic strength but it was also important to have sufficient troops ashore to hold the expected German counter-attack and continue to enlarge the beachhead. Landing behind the Canadians and the leading elements of 103 Beach Group, was 51st Highland Infantry Division. Badly delayed by the slower than planned establishment of the beachhead, 1 Gordon Highlanders waded ashore, late on the afternoon of D Day, as the leading element of 153 Brigade. Robert Rogge of 5 Black Watch was following them:

'Up on the deck, wearing all of our equipment and life belts, we could see the shore and Bernières-sur-Mer. It was Juno Beach. The 7th and 8th Brigades of our 3rd Canadian Infantry Division had already gone ashore. We went in very slowly, and as we got in closer, we could see a lot of stuff floating in the water and a few bodies. The craft just sort of stopped with a thump, and some of the guys fell down, and we had to pick them up again with all of that gear on them.

'The ship's crew dropped the ramps and we went on down and got into that water, and it was cold. I went in as far as my armpits, and while I was wading in to shore I could hear one of our pipers playing "Bonnie Dundee" on the ship behind us, and we were really getting piped into action. It was something. We could hear a lot of firing in the distance, and we waded ashore and there was a breach in the seawall, and movement control people herded us through the breach and up on into the town, where there were a lot of French people standing around, just looking at us.'

During the course of the evening, 153 Brigade concentrated at Banville, four miles inland, while for the next two days the remainder of the Division gained additional, unwelcome, 'sea-time' waiting for their turn to land on the congested beach.

Mike Red beach. A self-propelled anti-aircraft gun alongside a knocked out DD covers landings in the afternoon of D Day.

Chapter 5

The Advance Inland

The Juno beachhead delineated by the five mile long line of objective Yew was reached between 0900 and 1100 hours depending on the degree of resistance faced by the various advancing Canadian battalions. However, long after Yew was reached, isolated individuals and pockets of Germans were still proving to be a deadly nuisance, along with the thousands of mines and obstacles that littered the beach and immediate hinterland. Leaving the 'hard crust of the Atlantic Wall' behind them, the leading Canadians set out to secure the intermediate objective – Elm.

The insertion, during March 1944, of 352nd Division into the sector of the coast, which included Omaha Beach and the western portion of Gold Beach, had halved 716th Coastal Division's frontage. This had allowed the Germans to establish a second line inland and give their defences some depth. However, this line, between two and four thousand yards behind the coastal strip, was thin and made up of field fortifications rather than the concrete casemates of the coastal *Wiederstandneste*. The second line behind Mike Beach was largely held by two or three companies of 441 *Ost* Battalion, while the second line inland from Nan beach consisted only of a strong point based on the Headquarters and Staff Company of II/736 Regiment at Tailleville and the ground defences around the Douvres radar station. These German companies tended to be positioned around important junctions and on ground of tactical importance with good fields of fire across the open country. While they had an essentially defensive role, in the German's traditional layered defence, they also had a counter-attack task. It has already been recorded that 8 *Kompanie* 736 Grenadiers had been spotted by aircraft and largely dispersed by naval gunfire while they were deployed in the open, searching for paratroopers, shortly after dawn. However, the full effect of this advantage had largely passed, by early afternoon.

With the assault companies, having secured the beachhead (Yew), the divisional scheme of manoeuvre was for the leading battalions' second wave to cross the 'secured' beach and, with armoured support from the DD tanks, advance inland. Subsequently, the reserve battalions of 7 and 8 Cdn Brigades were to complete the advance to objectives on Elm. Meanwhile, assembling in the beachhead, 9 Cdn Brigade would complete Phase III of the divisional plan by securing Objective Oak, which lay along the line of the Caen Bayeux railway some ten miles inland. Phase IV (to be completed on D+1) would see the consolidation of the division along this line by the move forward by 7 and 8 Brigades. During Phases III and IV, if the

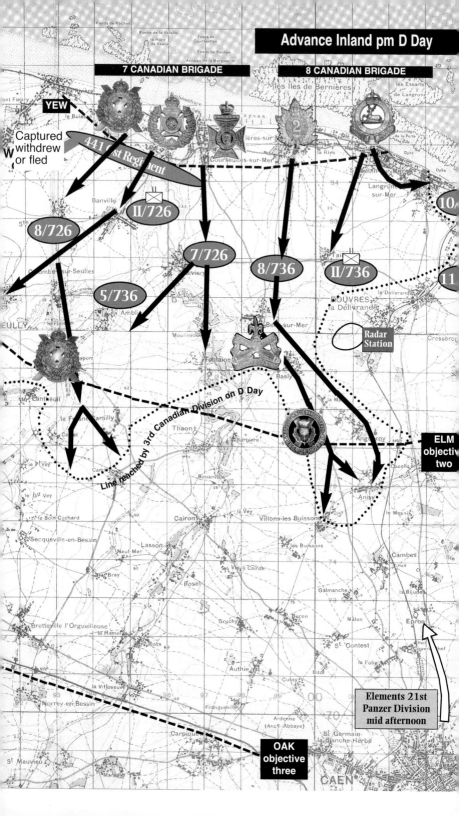

opportunity presented itself, strong patrols, in the form of tanks of the Canadian armoured regiments and the armoured cars of the Corps Recce Regiment would be pushed forward to objective around Hill 112 and on the river south of Caen. It must be stressed that, by D Day, these exploitation tasks were regarded very much as contingency plans.

7 Cdn Brigade's Advance Inland

The fight to overcome the defences along the open beaches and dunes of Mike Sector took 'a full two hours but ... by this time, some infantry groups were already far inland and substantial progress had been made towards the next objective' However, Objective Yew was only fully secured at H+4 hours.

The Brigade's first problem was a line of villages on the crest of the ridge looking down towards the beachhead: from left to right Reviers, Banville and St Croix. On the brigade's right, C Company, 1 Canadian Scottish were not involved in a major fighting through a coastal strong point or clearance of a coastal village and were, consequently, quickly through the Atlantic Wall. Their initial advance inland against the *Osttrupen* of 441 Battalion, was relatively easy as the enemy had been badly **See map on page 123** dislocated by the naval and air bombardment in the Vaux area. 1 Canadian Scottish recorded details of C Company's attack on St Croix in their after action report:

> '... platoons were unable to move up at this time due to heavy fire. The Coy was in a serious position with enemy infiltrating through our flanks. Wireless contact with the Bn was now established and it was found that they were well to our rear and not immediately available, but they managed to contact a squadron of DD tanks, which immediately came up to our assistance. The enemy seemed to be completely surprised at our appearance and many of them got out of their slit trenches and ran without firing another shot.
>
> 'Also at this time, Capt Brown, the artillery Forward Observation Officer with our party managed to get an arty concentration down on the enemy ... In this short engagement, another forty prisoners were taken, bringing our total to sixty-five, 6 MGs and one 105mm gun.
>
> 'A final word must be added giving credit to the stretcher bearers who worked fearlessly under the most trying conditions and were never found wanting when the cry for help went up.'

Eventually reinforced by the Winnipeg's A Company from the second wave, at about 0900 hours, the Canadian Scots were moving on and clearing St Croix-sur-Mer, which despite the bombardment was stoutly held by 8 *Kompanie* 726 Grenadiers.

A Canadian infantry company's tactical HQ prepares to move inland on the afternoon of D Day.

C Company of the Winnipegs had also been spared a major battle on the beach and was through Graye-sur-Mer and advancing on Banville, ignoring their open flanks. The Winnipegs' war diary records that they,

> '*...encountered several pockets of* [Osttrupen] *resistance en route but overcame each one until just south of Banville, where the enemy had dug in three MGs on commanding ground.*'

The diarist continues that having 'reached just short of assaulting distance before they were pinned down... the resistance was much stronger than intelligence had estimated'. In fact, Banville was the location of Major Lehmann's Battalion Headquarters of II/726 Grenadiers and his HQ Staff *Kompanie,* who were holding their ground despite suffering heavily from the Allied bombardment.

Meanwhile, D Company, the Winnipeg's battalion reserve, and the Commanding Officer's party were moving up on Banville from Graye-sur-Mer to join C Company. According to the battalions war diarist, 'Throughout this advance all sub units and Bn HQ had come under mortar and artillery fire of astonishing accuracy'. However, the battalion by now had the support of not only the mortars and medium machine guns of the

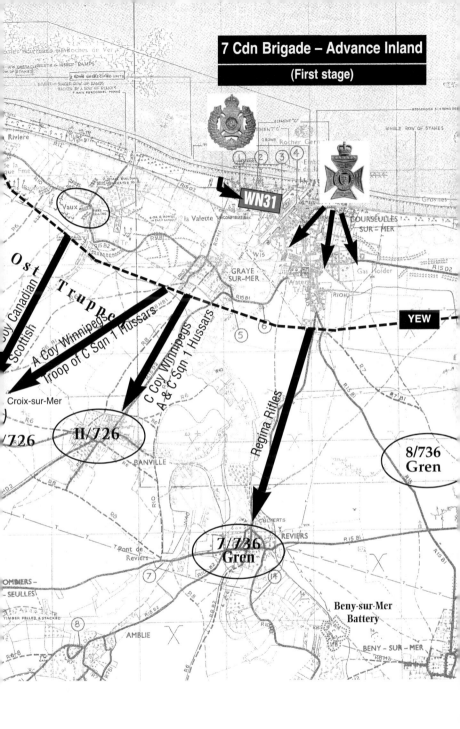

WN31

YEW

COURSEULLES-SUR-MER

GRAYE-SUR-MER

Gas Holder

Vaux

la Valette

Riviere

Ost Truppe

Coy Canadian Scottish

A Coy Winnipegs
Troop of C Sqn 1 Hussars

Croix-sur-Mer

C Coy Winnipegs
A & C Sqn 1 Hussars

Regina Rifles

II/726

/726

BANVILLE

Pont de Reviers

REVIERS

7/736
Gren

8/736
Gren

Beny-sur-Mer
Battery

BENY – SUR – MER

OMBIERS –
SEULLES

AMBLIE

123

Cameron Highlanders of Ottawa but also the self-propelled guns of 12th and 13th Canadian Field Regiments, who came into action on the edge of Courseulles. Fire from these units took some time to coordinate but once the enemy position was neutralised, the 'Little Black Devils' C and D Companies were able to cover the open ground and clear the machine guns and continue on to the village. Until 1310 hours, when Banville fell, the Winnipegs were still only two miles from the beach.

Initially the delay in opening vehicle gaps off Mike Beach had denied the infantry of 7 Cdn Brigade vital armoured support and the initial promising, but unsupported, advance slowed the tempo of operations to a crawl – almost literally amongst the inland villages. Some time later, an entry in the battalion war diary records how:

> 'Portions of A and C Squadrons 6 Cdn Armd Regt [1st Hussars] *went to the help of A Company* [Winnipegs] *with cool disregard for mines and A-tk guns, beat down the MG positions and permitted A Coy to mop up and advance to the south.'*

It could be expected that now a combined arms battle (infantry, tanks and guns) was being fought progress would be quicker. However, the stoutly built village buildings, complimented by dugouts and shelters were difficult to clear and a few determined defenders tied down large numbers of infantry. This was the case in Banville where, despite being overrun and Major Lehmann being killed, at HQ II/726 Grenadiers, 'The Adjutant defended the HQ bunker with a handful of men until nightfall. Then they fought their way out.' The difference between the *Osttruppen,* who largely melted away at the first opportunity and a degree of determination amongst the coastal infantry, is marked. What is often forgotten is that the coastal divisions were leavened with combat experienced officers and NCOs.

Meanwhile, also exploiting the break through on the right flank, were the remainder of the Canadian Scottish (7 Cdn Brigade's reserve battalion), who as recorded in the official history: '... was able to start its move across the grain fields towards St Croix-sur-Mer.' This advance included D Company, who were equipped with bicycles, which had been provided to some infantry companies for use in what planners hoped to be a mobile battle. They 'headed up an exit off the beach, across an open field, which was under MG fire, to secure to secure two bridges over the sur Seulles' beyond St Croix-sur-Mer. Bicycles, as obsolescent as cavalry in these circumstances were understandably and promptly abandoned as a viable means of battlefield mobility. D Company platoons fanned out to seize and hold the bridges, completing most of their advance on foot.

The official history records that the Canadian Scottish continued its move inland and:

> '... *En route it picked up its C Company, which had landed in the*

A 105mm Priest battery in action on D Day.

A Canadian gunner stands guard in front of his 105mm Priest SP gun.

assault wave. There were a considerable number of casualties from machine gun fire during the advance, which was pushed with all possible speed. After dealing with snipers [more properly 'isolated riflemen'] *in St Croix the battalion continued its movement to the Seulles crossing of the village.'*

With St Croix taken by the combined efforts of the two battalions and six tanks of C Squadron 1st Hussars, the Winnipeg's next objective was, the village of Creully. Lieutenant Battershill, in command of Number 7 Platoon, however, had an important mission,

'to be dispatched to our right to join up with a like sized force from the British [50th Division] *to form a strong point on the boundary between our two divisions to detect and stop any attempts at counter-attack ...'*

at this traditionally weak point. Lieutenant Battershill's platoon, who in a damaged craft, had landed on their own in the area between the Canadians and British wrote:

'After the initial landing and being in a strange land with only map references to guide us, we took some time to make contact with the rest of A Company. After a period of orientation with the Company [in St Croix sur Mer], *we set off to find our rendezvous point with a British platoon on our right on the eastern outskirts of Cruelly. We established a platoon defensive position and were pleased to find that we were in the right place as we were contacted by the British soon after. We ... consolidated our position, patrolled, and were on the lookout for any sign of enemy activity. A small number of prisoners were taken and processed through the British.'*

On the left flank, as has already been described, the Reginas' initial assault wave was committed to capturing WN 29 at Courseulles East and to clearing the town. Meanwhile, having led the second wave through the town, D Company advanced towards Reviers. According to Colonel Stacey,

'The leading elements reached the village at about 1100 hours; by 1215 hours it was reported by C Company, which had followed D from Courseulles that the bridges in Reviers were secured'.

The capture of these bridges, defended by 7 *Kompanie* 726 Grenadiers, intact was a significant achievement and A Company was left behind to guard the important crossings of the Seulles and Mue Rivers. The remainder of the battalion fanned out to advance to the villages of Fontaine-Henry and Le Fresne-Camilly. These villages were reached by early evening.

With St Croix, Banville and Reviers taken 7 Cdn Brigade, and it's supporting tank squadrons from 1/Hussars were through the main German defences and progress was relatively easy but slow. The enemy

D Company Regina Rifles advancing through Reviers on D-Day.

defences were based on anti-tank guns deployed in depth and infantry belonging to II/726 Grenadiers and 441 *Ost battalion*, who had been forced out of their positions just inland from the beach.

From mid-morning, once they had struggled through the tenuous gaps off the beach, the squadrons of 1 Hussars had each supported one of 7 Cdn Brigade's infantry battalions. Due to the slow concentration inland, the squadrons had initially deployed their tanks in troop sized groups in answer to the calls of the pinned down infantry. To compound their losses on the beach and amongst the coastal minefields, the advance inland reduced the Hussars' strength to the point that A and B Squadrons between them had lost eighteen tanks. Most of the losses were attributed during this phase to German anti-tank guns sited on the inland ridges and to protective minefields around the defended villages.

The Canadian official historian recorded that in 7 Cdn Brigade's area:

> 'The enemy's rear area was overwhelmed by our infantry, and the tanks of 6 Cdn Armoured Regiment [1 Hussars], once clear of the coastal inundations, found his staff cars and light vehicles easy targets.'

Having fought much of the morning with amongst or behind the Winnipegs, the Canadian Scottish advanced south east from St Croix towards the villages of Colombiers-sur-Seulles and Pierrepont, of which the latter lay along the line of Objective Elm. The battalion war diary states that they:

> '... advanced with little or no opposition. However, from the

number of enemy wounded and dead found during the advance, there was proof that the enemy had once controlled that area. Upon arriving in Colombiers, further proof of the enemy's rapid retreat was evident. Up until our entrance into the town, the Germans had had their [company] HQ here but they left in full retreat leaving their typewriter and office supplies behind them.

'The Battalion carried on through the town after sampling various wines and ciders brought to them by the local inhabitants.'

Pleased to be taken prisoner, two men from an *Ost* battalion.

8 Cdn Brigade's Advance Inland

The many delays inflicted on the Canadians who landed on Nan Sector, were not only the result of the delays and stronger than anticipated resistance at *Wiederstandnest* 27 and 28 but was also the result of congestion in the coastal towns. As has already been recorded, 9 Cdn Brigade had started to land shortly after 1100 hours but found themselves bunched up in Bernières, while the Queen's Own Rifles of Canada and the Regiment de Chaudiere broke out of the town and headed inland. A series of entries in the QOR of C war diary describe the slow process of the break out:

'0940 hours. There is considerable delay at this point while the companies assemble. B Coy's casualties being so heavy they gather just off the beach and try to sort themselves out. A Coy having extricated themselves from the position on the right flank proceed to their Forming up Point. The Regt de Chaud have now landed but are prevented from passing through us by the very accurate fire of a battery of 88mm guns located just south of Bernières sur Mer.'

With the well concealed *Spandaus* of 8 *Kompanie* 736 Grenadiers and supporting anti-tank guns in a well developed defensive position on the high ground south of Bernières, any movement out of the village was impossible until the enemy were neutralised by fire. The Queen's Own's C Company was pinned down at the edge of Bernières by long range fire and was unable to cross the open fields behind the town. The supporting tanks of the Fort Garry Horse were also brought to a halt by a pair of anti-tank

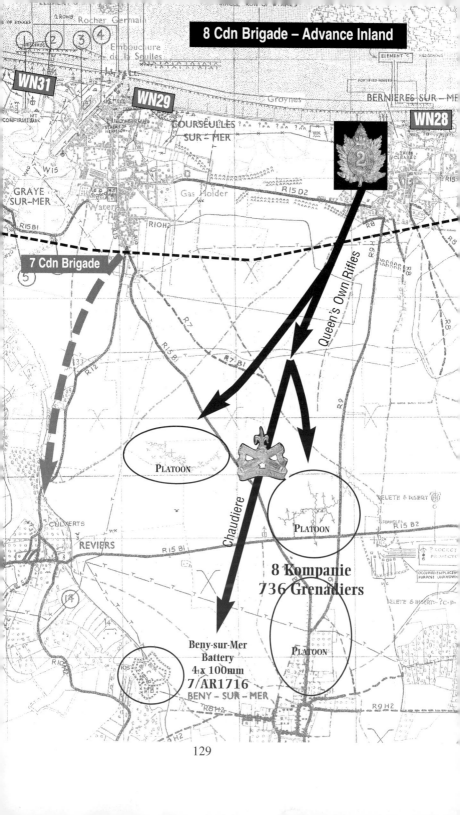

8 Cdn Brigade – Advance Inland

WN31

WN29

BERNIERES-SUR-MER

WN28

COURSEULLES
SUR-MER

GRAYE
SUR-MER

7 Cdn Brigade

Queen's Own Rifles

PLATOON

PLATOON

Chaudiere

REVIERS

8 Kompanie
736 Grenadiers

PLATOON

Beny-sur-Mer
Battery
4 x 100mm
7/AR1716
BENY – SUR – MER

129

guns covering the slopes rising up to Bény-sur-Mer. 716 Division is recorded as having two batteries of anti-tank guns; a battery of ten guns on self-propelled mounts and a further battery of eleven towed guns, of which two were 88s and the remainder 75mm Pak 40s. Some of the towed guns were deployed on the coast to supplement the obsolescent 50mm guns at key points. However, accounts estimate that about twelve anti-tank guns were operational across the divisional front. Amongst those pinned down on the edge of the village was Rifleman Bull Ross who wrote:

'There was heavy congestion of equipment. Some vehicles were directed to go left into an apple orchard. On the right of the road tanks and self propelled guns moved into a hayfield. Several tanks had taken hits. An 88mm [probably a 75mm] emplacement was well sited about half a mile ahead of us. Lt Col Jock Spragge called for smoke, the mortars laid down a smokescreen that blocked the Germans view. The tanks were blowing up. The crews inside were screaming. Shreds of tank metal were flying around everywhere. A German machine gun in a trench on the right began to spray us. Just behind me, an artillery observation officer had been trying to find where the 88mm was located; he was hit by a burst of fire. Eventually a section of our men co-ordinated with one of the tanks and they cleaned out the 88mm and captured a number of prisoners. But we suffered a lot of casualties from that machine gun on the right and the 88 up ahead on our left.'

Colonel Stacey noted that: 'The Armour and infantry were held up for nearly two hours until our artillery and medium machine guns could silence the opposition. Then the infantry was gradually infiltrated up the road from Bernières towards Bény-sur-Mer.' Under heavy bombardment,

Men of the Chaudiere Regiment moving through Bernières to the inland battle.

Regiment de la Chaudiere.

with tanks and infantry closing in the German defence waivered and broke. In clearing the enemy position, the QOR of C had been ordered by Brigadier Blackadder to go beyond Objective Yew and onto what should have been the Chaudiere's initial objective but the latter battalion was still

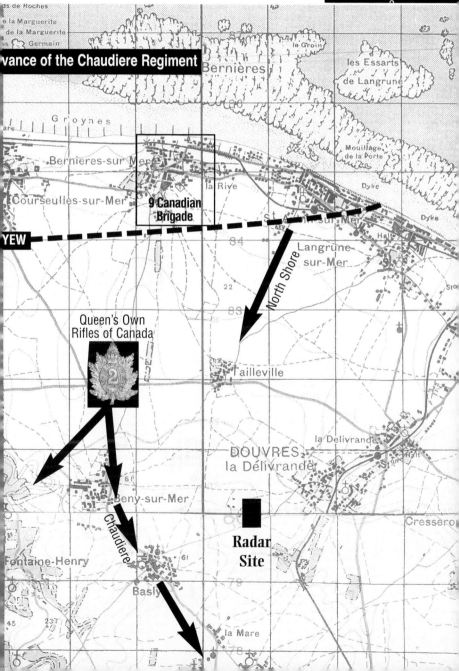

Advance of the Chaudiere Regiment

9 Canadian Brigade

YEW

Queen's Own Rifles of Canada

North Shore

Chaudiere

Radar Site

moving up and the Queen's Own had the initiative and combat power to do the job. The QOR of C battalion's war diarist continued:

> '1000 hours. *The 88 battery having been finally taken care of, the Regt de Chaud move ahead followed at a discreet distance by our C and D Coys mounted on the tanks and other available vehicles.*
>
> '1400 hours. *Several stops on the road before Beny-sur-Mer is clear enough to move in. Here there was more delay while the Regt de Chaud went on to capture Basly.*'

The exact time at which Bény and its artillery battery was cleared of the enemy is not recorded but the Regiment de Chaudiere reported that they were advancing south from Bény towards Basly at 1530 hours and shortly afterwards that 'Forward companies reported themselves in Basly'. German resistance had clearly not crumbled with the capture of Bény, as it had taken the Chaudiere nearly an hour and a half to advance less than a mile, even with the support of the Shermans of the Fort Garry Horse.

On 8 Brigade's left flank, it will be recalled that *Wiederstandneste* 27 in St Aubin was the North Shore Regiment's main problem, which had monopolized B Company's attention for most of the day. However, A

Soldiers of the Chaudiere Regiment photographed waiting to advance on D Day.

The open country across which the North Shore advanced.

Company had crossed the beach and made good progress inland, reporting that they had pushed on and had approached Tailleville during Phase 1 (the assault Phase). Despite this early promise, taking this village, which was the Headquarters of II/736 Regiment and largely held by the Battalion's Staff *Kompanie*, was to take a considerable time.

Captain Le Blanc, Second in Command of C Company, a part of the North Shore's second wave, assembled in St Aubin in good order having suffered few casualties:

> *'The advance started on toward Tailleville, our objective. As we were advancing with one platoon on the right and another on the left, with men spread out into the fields, the enemy mortars opened up. Sergeant Girvan came running back wounded in the neck. He was evacuated after being given first aid, then casualty reports started coming from the platoons. The tanks gave us good support so we kept slowly moving ahead.'*

Also advancing south from St Aubin was tank troop commander Lieutenant Little of the Fort Garry Horse, who could see up to a hundred enemy soldiers of 736 Regiment withdrawing from the coastal defences:

> *'The excitement was just fantastic, and I called my other tank and pointed out the target and said, "let them have it!" It was a real bird-shoot. We caught them in the open, with all the guns. The exhilaration after all the years of training, the tremendous feeling of lift, excitement exhilaration, of doing this! It was like the first time you had gone deer hunting, and the deer had come out. You quivered with excitement.'*

133

However, as infantry and tanks closed in on Tailleville enemy fire increased and the advance ground to a halt. Meanwhile, with the majority of his force ashore, Major General Keller left the headquarter ship HMS *Hilary* with his Tactical Headquarters at 1145 hours to join his troops in what was now a reasonably secure beachhead. Landing at Bernières, he was joined some two hours later by the first part of 'Div Main HQ' and the first headquarters of the campaign was established in an orchard on the outskirts of the village. Having established communications, an angry General Keller called for three of his brigadiers (8, 9 and 2 Armoured Brigades) to consider the difficulty and consequent delays that the division was experiencing in advancing on its left flank. The divisional war diary confirms that,

> 'No change of plan was ordered: 8 Cdn Inf Bde was still to capture Beny-sur-Mer, after which 9 Cdn Inf Bde could be passed through on its axis towards Carpiquet.'

General Keller was extremely frustrated that the situation, which had seemed favourable when he decided to land 9 Cdn Brigade on Nan Beach, had turned sour, but with the River Seulles on the brigade's right flank he had little option but to persist with his original plan.

With the North Shore's A Company having now been joined by C and D Companies to the north of Tailleville, they found that,

> 'The defenders were well dug in and provided with an extensive system of tunnels which gave excellent opportunities to snipers'.

General Keller and staff ashore near the D Day house.

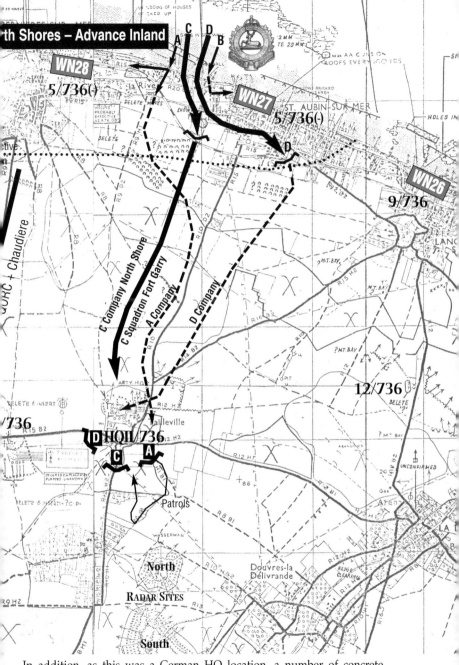

In addition, as this was a German HQ location, a number of concrete positions and shelters had been built. Stiffened by the presence of the battalion commander and sheltered by the stout buildings, and concrete strengthened cellars, the Germans put up a good and protracted fight. In

135

doing so they showed that well led, and with a little luck, in that they had missed the worst of the Allied fire plan, coastal troops in soundly prepared positions, could be effective against the best assault troops. Even when defeat was inevitable they fought on. The last message from Headquarters II/736 Grenadiers in Tailleville, timed 1548 hours, is recorded in the regimental war diary: 'Hand-to-hand fighting inside the command post. We are hemmed into a closely confined area, but still holding out.'

C Company, eventually crushed the main centre of resistance during an attack launched at 1800 hours, with the support of thirteen Shermans. About fifty prisoners were taken at the cost of fourteen Canadians killed,

PM D Day, the Canadians have dug-in are ready to fight 21st Panzer Division.

including a company commander, Major MacNaughton. However, the fighting to clear the village and surrounding areas went on until 2100 hours, with the engineers deploying their man-pack flamethrowers to eliminate the final pockets of resistance. The enemy who fought on at Tailleville, in contrast with the majority of *Osttruppen* further west in the divisional area, prevented the North Shores from advancing to clear the Douvres radar station or from reaching Objective Elm. The fight to clear the radar station is covered in Chapter 7. It must be recognized that the delay imposed on the 3rd Canadian Division by II/736 Grenadiers at Tailleville contributed significantly to their failure to reach their objective on the Caen-Bayeux Road on D Day. The fight at Tailleville also provides an insight into what would have faced the Allied invaders had Rommel had the time and resources to build a substantial second line, rather than rely on troops who were mainly occupying field fortifications.

Oberleutnant Werner Fieberg, escaped capture at Tailleville. He recorded that:

> *'The strong point was overrun by the British. I only avoided capture, as I was away from the headquarters to visit our artillery observers. We had no rations and little ammunition or material, so we waited until dusk, and once darkness had fallen, tried to get past English positions, patrols and bivouacs, and break through to our lines. Our progress was slow as the enemy was everywhere and after four days, my group was laying in a coma, exhausted, having hardly anything to eat or drink in the meantime, we were discovered and taken prisoner'*

The Advance to Objective Elm and Beyond

With the Germans holding out at Tailleville on the Division's left flank, the QOR of C and the Chaudiere continued their advance from Bény-sur-Mer and Basly to Colomby-sur-Thaon and Anguerny, followed by 9 Cdn Brigade. The main German resistance had been broken and the Canadian advance was now opposed by small groups of enemy troops, some of whom were conducting a fighting withdrawal, while others fired in the hope of keeping the Canadians at a respectable distance while they escaped. With objective Elm reached, Colonel Stacey recorded that 9 Cdn Brigade took over the lead from the QOR of C and the Chaudiere and advanced towards the northern outskirts of Caen and the Carpiquet airfield:

See map on page 139

> *'9 Cdn Inf Bde did not encounter serious resistance until it reached Villong-les-Buissons, some four miles from Caen. Here the leading battalion (North Nova Scotia Highlanders) was held up by troublesome machine gun positions.'*

Further west, in 7 Cdn Brigade's area, the Regina Rifles advanced from

Canadian commanders and signallers from 2 Armoured Brigade monitor the progress of the battle.

Reviers towards Fontaine-Henry and just about reached objective Elm. In the circumstances, this was a very good achievement for a battalion that had assaulted Nan Green, cleared Courseulles and broken the German second line at Revieres. On the division's right flank, 7 Cdn Brigade's reserve battalion, the Canadian Scottish took over from the Winnipegs and surged across Elm towards Cainet and Camily. Meanwhile, elements of 2 Cdn Armoured Brigade were fanning out ahead taking advantage of the absence of anti-tank guns now that they were through the enemy second line. In addition, there were no enemy tanks reported. 3rd Canadian Division's summary of operations recorded that:

> 'Two troops of 6 Cdn Armd Regt [1st Hussars] *had actually penetrated to the final objective* [Oak] *near Bretteville but after*

destroying many of the enemy, withdrew without loss'. These two tank troops and others had advanced on their own without support and, consequently found themselves isolated without infantry support. Vulnerable to attack by enemy armed with Panzerfausts, *they withdrew back to positions with the infantry who were pinned down by pockets of enemy resistance based on machine guns.'*

This early incident points to the criticism later levelled at both British and Canadians that their armour and infantry while 'co-operating' on the same battlefield, tended to fight their own battle.

Although in action for over ten hours, 7 Cdn Brigade had done well and the Canadian Scottish were clearly through the organized enemy defences. 9 Cdn Brigade had also only deployed one of its battalions and arguably had plenty of combat power. However, tiredness, the earlier delays and a certain amount of 'confusion of battle' was capped by intelligence indications descending the chain of command that the 'panzers were coming'. This brought the day's advance inland to a halt. Rather than fighting to hold *ad hoc* positions along the line of Objective Oak, south of the Caen Bayeux Road, the Canadians would defend their gains where

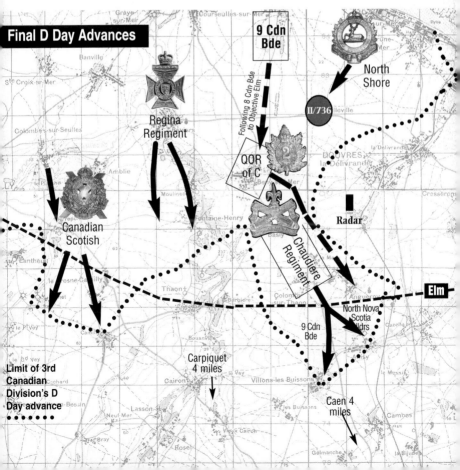

Final D Day Advances

9 Cdn Bde

North Shore

II/736

Regina Regiment

Following 8 Cdn Bde to Objective Elm

QOR of C

DOUVRES la Délivrande

Radar

Canadian Scottish

Chaudiere Regiment

Elm

North Nova Scotia Hldrs

9 Cdn Bde

Carpiquet 4 miles

Caen 4 miles

Limit of 3rd Canadian Division's D Day advance

A panzer MkIV of 21st Panzer Division breaks cover.

Canadian Bren gun crew guard approaches to the landings.

they stood. The infantry dug in and the anti-tank guns were brought forward.

21st Panzer Division West of Caen

As a result of his experiences at the hands of the Allied airforces in the Mediterranean, *Generalfeldmarshall* Rommel argued that he needed the vital panzer formation, within immediate striking distance of the coast, if he was to repel an invasion. However, C in C West, *Generalfeldmarshall* von Rundstedt, disagreed and supported the conventional view of identifying the enemy's main effort before concentrating to strike, while leaving coastal formations to contain and reduce the invader's combat power. Exponents of both opinions appealed to the Führer, who promptly ordered that the majority of the panzer troops were not to be committed without his personal authority. Consequently neither side prevailed and the German commanders were left with a chaotic solution that suited neither opinion.

Generalmajor Edgar Feuchtinger, commander of 21st Panzer Division.

Rommel was given command of just three panzer divisions, of which the 21st (of *Afrikakorps* fame) was located between Caen and Falaise. The rest of the panzer divisions remained under HQ *Panzergruppe* West, with two divisions, Panzer *Lehr* and 12th *Hitlerjugend* SS Panzer Division, being twelve to forty-eight hours march from the invasion coast. However, as the armoured reserve, they could only be committed with Hitler's authority. Matters were further complicated by the fact that the *Hitlerjugend* was under SS command rather than the *Wehrmacht*.

Fearing the early intervention of panzers, Montgomery had amended the OVERLORD plan, widening the invasion front to some sixty miles, in order to dissipate the German response. From the outset German reserves marched to both flanks to counter the airborne landings. Around Caen, the 21st's panzer grenadiers were quickly in action against 6th Airborne Division and 22 Panzer Regiment, having been alerted at 0100 hours, was marching to join them, harried as they drove north by Allied fighter-bombers. However, before they came into contact the situation changed and *Generalmajor* Feuchtinger was instructed that his *schwerepunkt* lay west of Caen. The panzers turned about and started to make their way through Caen's suburbs. At 1300 hours, Feuchtinger again halted his columns. This time to regroup his command into three *Kampfgruppen* based on his three regiments (each equivalent to an Anglo/Canadian brigade). 125 Panzer Grenadier Regiment (125 Pz Gr Regt) or as it was known *Kampfgruppe* von Luck, were directed back through Caen to attack 6th Airborne Division. The division's other two *Kampfgruppen* were to attack the British beachheads west of Caen. One *Kampfgruppen* was heavy armour, with two panzer and one infantry battalions, and the other, *Kampfgruppe* Rauch, based on 192 Pz Gr Regt, had a single panzer battalion but two infantry battalions. The regrouping took two hours, as the marching and counter-marching had inflicted its usual mechanical vehicle casualties in addition to losses from Allied air interdiction. *Oberst* von Luck wrote:

> 'The regrouping of the division took hours. Most of the units, from the area east of Caen and the Orne had to squeeze through the eye of a needle at Caen and over the only bridges available in this sector. Caen was under virtually constant bombardment from the navy and fighter bombers of the RAF.'

The importance of 21st Panzer Division's mission is underlined by the presence of General Marcks, the Corps Commander, who personally led *Kampfgruppe* Rauch into its assembly area. The division was to drive a wedge between the Sword and Juno lodgements and drive the enemy back into the sea. At 1620 hours, the two *Kampfgruppen* advanced northwards. *Kampfgruppe* Rauch was on the left heading towards the coast and 3rd Canadian Division.

General Erich Marcks.

These tactical delays were exacerbated by failure of German operational command to release the other panzer divisions. Von Rundstedt had given the *Hitlerjugend* and Panzer *Lehr* orders to move at dawn hours, believing that his common sense order would be confirmed by OKW. However, Hitler had not been woken with news of the landings and, at 0600 hours, OKW 'angrily countermanded von Rundstedt's release the panzers'. The tank crews who had rushed to their vehicles as code words were telephoned around divisional areas now waited, as rumour circulated and Allied aircraft could be seen dominating the sky above them. It was well after mid-day when Hitler eventually awoke and was briefed.

It is wrong to entirely attribute the delay as a result in releasing the *Panzergruppe* West's armoured reserves to the failure to wake Hitler before dawn. In German headquarters in France and Berlin, the legitimate question was 'Is this the real invasion?' Thanks to the highly successful deception operation, FORTITUDE, the Germans had vastly overestimated the number of Allied divisions waiting in England. The commitment of three airborne divisions out of what the Germans incorrectly estimated was nine such divisions, even if supported by amphibious landings, could well have been designed to enduce them to deploy their scant reserves. It

North Nova Scotia Highlanders radio operator. Photographed on the afternoon of D Day.

was only by late morning that it was confirmed that elements of seven Allied infantry divisions had landed in the first wave and the Germans were convinced that this was more than merely a raid on a grand scale. The problem is very well summarised by SS *Sturmbannführer* Hayn who was a member of the *Hitlerjugend's* intelligence staff:

> '... the minutes dragged by. One individual report followed another; they confirmed or contradicted each other. Army or Army Group HQ were constantly telephoning. But all the Corps staff could do was to wait — wait until the confused overall picture had been clarified, until the main centres of the dropping and landing zones had become apparent.'

However, in the case of 21st Panzer Division, it was the confusion of battle, rather than the deliberations of the high command that had delayed the delivery of coherent orders. Under pressure, commanders were forced to make decisions based on incomplete and often wrong information. Consequently, as recorded above, Generals

With the armoured threat approaching, the armoured tank regiment's guns were brought forward.

Feuchtinger and Marcks had 21st Panzer Division marching and counter-marching in the Caen area for most of the day. Montgomery's plan had successfully prevented the enemy from being able to intervene at the decisive point and at the decisive time. It is an often forgotten fact that the fundamentally sound OVERLORD plan was one of the most significant factors in the D Day victory.

As has already been recorded, situation reports warning of the approach of 21st Panzer Division had started to descend the 3rd Canadian Division's chain of command during the late afternoon. This had the effect of halting the Canadians' advance inland, as commanders sought to balance their forces to withstand a counter-attack, rather than push headlong to their final objectives. The infantry's battle procedure changed from offensive to defensive. Forward companies were halted, if possible in advantageous positions, while following companies and units closed up to add depth to defences. Commanders' highest priorities were to co-ordinate the anti-tank plan. 2nd Armoured Brigade went into positions where they could counter-attack any enemy penetrations. The self-propelled and towed guns of the anti-tank regiment were positioned covering the main armoured approaches, while the 6-pounders of the infantry battalions covered other approaches and the spring loaded Projector Infantry Anti-

The Cameron Highlanders of Ottawa brought up their medium machine guns and mortars to hold the ground gained.

Tank (PIAT) were deployed to give defence against panzers to individual infantry platoons.

Meanwhile, on the coastal strip, Lieutenant Colonel Moulton and 48 Commando Royal Marines, having been checked at the enemy strong point in Lagrune-sur-Mer and gone into defensive positions to contain the German defenders of WN 26 for the night, now faced inland as well. **See Chapter 6**

In the event, 3rd British Division's defences shaped the enemy armoured *Kampfgrupen's* drive to the sea and the panzers drove into the gap between the Allies' Juno and Sword lodgements. Other than recce and flank protection detachments, little of 21st Panzer Division came into serious contact with the Canadians. However, at 2100 hours, in the last hour of daylight, 'a hush fell over the battlefield', as a distant hum grew into a great throbbing wall of sound. Fleets of Allied transport aircraft appeared on the horizon. Lines of parachutes bloomed in the sky and gliders swept down in Landing Zone in the area of Ouisterham. *Unteroffizier* Kortenhaus watched from the turret of a Panzer IV:

> '...no one who saw it can forget. Suddenly the hollow roaring of countless aeroplanes, and then we saw them, hundreds of them, towing great gliders, filling the sky.... The sky was full of colour, flame and falling objects, and it was impossible to know where to look.'

The effect of this overwhelming display of air power on German morale was immediate. Not least because the panzers had already been confronted, as they came down the ridge towards the coast, with a seascape crammed with shipping of all sorts and sizes, and now they seemed in danger of being cut off by airborne forces. Morale hit and lacking sufficient infantry, 21st Panzer Division was not going to be able to maintain the battle overnight, the Germans broke off the engagement and withdrew.

Conclusion

Many have commented on the failure of the Allies to reach their D Day objectives. In the case of the British and Canadian divisions of Second Army, it was appreciated at the time that taking Caen and the deployment of armoured patrols south towards the high ground of Hill 112 was ambitious. However, a commander needs to set challenging objectives and have plans ready to help exploit any opportunity presented by the enemy.

While the Allies may not have reached their objectives, *Generallieutenant* Richter, estimated that 716th Division lost four-fifths of its infantry strength on D Day. '...of four German and two Russian battalions there remained in the evening one German battalion which had had about twenty percent casualties; otherwise only remnants.' Colonel Stacey recorded that 'Eighty per cent of the German artillery was gone; west of the Orne two batteries were left, each with three guns'. The division had been taken apart by the Allies and it had all but ceased to exist. However, on Juno Beach, with the delay between the end of the heaviest part of the fire plan and the landing, the Germans had fought creditably and 'gave a good return'.

This return was in the form of Canadian and British dead and wounded, 'which though heavy, were fewer than had been feared'. However, it is difficult to make an authoritative statement of the casualties suffered by those landing on Juno Beach on D Day. In common with every other beach, the bulk of the casualties fell to the assault infantry battalions. For instance, the QORC lost 143 men and the Winnipegs 128 casualties and the North Shores 125. In total 3rd Canadian Division lost 275 all ranks killed, 539 wounded and about fifty taken prisoner, which gives a total just short of a thousand. To this must be added the losses suffered by the Navy and Royal Marine landing craft crews, 48 Commando and the assault troops of 79th Armoured Division and, last but not least, 103 Beach Group and 51st Highland Division. This gives a D Day figure of approaching 2,000 casualties for Juno Beach.

Chapter 6

St Aubin to Lagrune-sur-Mer

Wiederstandneste 27, at the eastern end of Nan Red Sector, formed a part of the North Shore Regiment's initial objective that had to be taken before moving inland towards Objective Yew. Landing behind the North Shore were the Royal Marine Commandos, in the form of 48 Commando and Headquarters 4 Special Service Brigade. While 48 landed, 46 Commando RM was to remain afloat as the Commando reserve, ready to be deployed anywhere on Second Army's front or on the Allied left flank in order to deal with batteries that had not been silenced by the naval or air bombardment.

48 Commando's task was not to strike inland but to fight its way from St Aubin eastward towards Sword Beach, where landing behind 3rd British Division, 41 Commando would be heading westward to meet them. The task of fighting an independent action, on a flank, to linking up the two beachheads, was never going to be an easy job, hence the commitment of commandos to the task. The gap between Sword and Juno was just less than five miles and included the coastal resort villages of St Aubin, Lagrune, Luc and Lion (all with the suffix 'sur-Mer'). Amongst these villages were a series of strong points held by the reinforced 9 *Kompanie* 736 Grenadier Regiment and a part of 10 *Kompanie*. The *Wiederstandneste* at Lagrune-sur-Mer, as forecast, proved to be well constructed and surprisingly determinedly held by the German coastal troops and *osttruppen*.

St Aubin-sur-Mer

It will be recalled that The North Shore's B Company had been held up by machine gun fire from WN 27 and that the strong point's 50mm guns knocked out the first tanks coming up onto the beach. An AVRE, after forty-five minutes fighting, 'cracked the concrete casemate with a "Dustbin" and took the sting out of the Germans'.

Wiederstandneste 27 had more or less fallen to B Company, after two hours of fighting, as described in Chapter 3. However, resistance from German infantry in the houses along the esplanade and in the village was to persist until 1800 hours and it was not until the following morning that an isolated group of *osttruppen* gunners finally surrendered.

The Germans who escaped from the strong point fell back into the village where, particularly to the east, some of the houses had been prepared for defence. These enemy infantry had been largely spared the

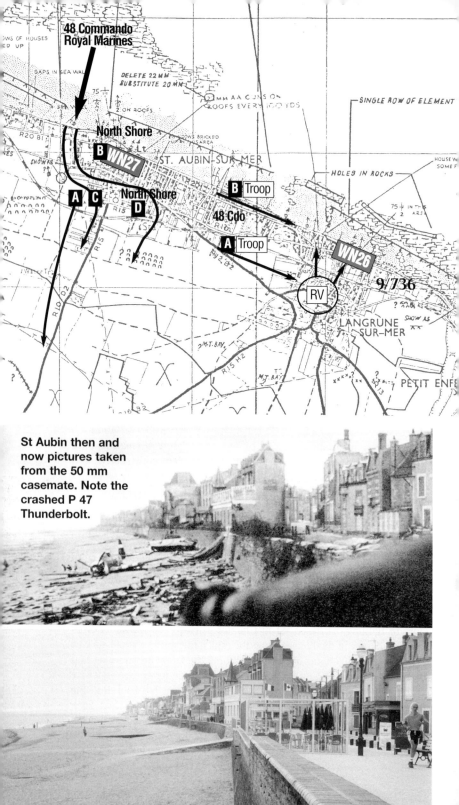

48 Commando Royal Marines

JWS OF HOUSES
CO UP

GAPS IN SEA WAL

DELETE 22 MM
SUBSTITUTE 20 MM

75

2 ON ROOFS

MM AA GUNS ON
ROOFS EVERY 100 YDS

SINGLE ROW OF ELEMENT

R20 B1

OWS BRICKED
AREA

North Shore

B WN27

ST. AUBIN-SUR-MER

HOLES IN ROCKS

HOUSE W
SOME F

A **C**

D

North Shore

R15

B Troop

48 Cdo

75 IN TH
2 ARE

A Troop

WN26

RV

9/736

LANGRUNE
SUR-MER

SHOW AS

PETIT ENF

2 M.T. BAY

R15 H2

M.T. BAY

St Aubin then and now pictures taken from the 50 mm casemate. Note the crashed P 47 Thunderbolt.

worst effects of the heavy bombardment and had seen the effects of their resistance on the Canadians whose tanks and men fell under their fire. However, those taking refuge in the coastal villas and terraces received some close range fire support from converted landing craft, while the Canadians attacked from the landward side.

The North Shore's history described the fighting in St Aubin and the problems faced by the soldiers from New Brunswick at WN27:

'*Major Bob Forbes* [Officer Commanding B Company] *needed some help for his troops, so a section of carriers was suggested to push along through alleyways and give his men cover to advance in attack. It was a slow procedure, but the carriers moved along, the anti-tank guns blazed and B Company cleared one building after another. They were joined together by underground passages and there was a system of trenches as well. We would get the Germans out of one tough spot and they would re-appear in another. We could not figure it out at the moment but by persistent fire and rushes B Company got them out and took a lot of prisoners. The pioneers were called and blew up a building that was in the way.*'

B Company's protracted battle in the area of WN 27 required them to clear the village, building by building, which contributed to the North Shore's lack of combat power to speedily overcome opposition when the remainder of the battalion advanced inland.

Meanwhile, C and D Companies, the reserve companies of the North Shore Regiment, left B Company to clear WN 27 and set out to clear the remainder of St Aubin. Amongst those making their way through the village was Gunner Johnston driving an M10 Tank Destroyer belonging to

A Sherman moving through the streets of St Aubin.

52nd Canadian Anti-Tank Battery. He described how having got off the beach and driven into St Aubin:

> 'I forget at what point we blew off our waterproofing, but we came into a corner, maybe one hundred yards, and we met the British commandos. We were about the first troops that they had run into and one of their officers said, in his British accent, "You have to turn left heah!" I looked and saw there were bodies lying on the road and I said, "Oh my God, not for a minute." I said, "We're gonna have to move some of those bodies because I am not going to run over any more of my own bodies today" The bodies were still warm, I know because we moved them. There were lots; I guess a machine gun nest or something caught them.

> 'We went round the corner – you have to realize I was only looking through a periscope sight and you can only see so far down – and came across a slit trench behind a pillbox. We dropped the muzzle of our 50 – calibre into the trench, gave it a couple of blasts and a couple of grenades and we heard 'Kamrade' and they was coming out. I don't know how many we killed but we took twenty-one men and an officer out of there as prisoners.

> 'The prisoners were shaken up pretty good. The order of the day was 'no quarter', that meant no prisoners to my way of thinking. So one of my buddies wanted to shoot them, ...but our officer was a good guy and he said, "No." So we took them back. These were the first prisoners we took. One of our guys, the gunner on our vehicle, had a Bren gun and every time these guys would slow down he'd let off the Bren over their heads and got their jackboot heels going like you wouldn't believe. By this time, the engineers were trying to build a PW compound and we brought these prisoners in there.'

Landing some minutes after the first wave, were the North Shore's reserve companies. Captain LeBlanc, second in command of C Company, recounted that the heavily laden men were born across the beach by a wave of adrenaline.

> 'We didn't have too many casualties on the beach, because we had made plans to get across as quickly as possible. I made a gap with my own wire-cutters along a wall and, after a reconnaissance, I told the platoons to follow me. Lieutenant MacQuarrie's and Lieutenant Fawcett's platoons followed me, with no casualties but Lieutenant Day's platoon had found another gap and in going through it suffered three casualties. We met Major Daughney where we should have and then all started working our way towards St Aubin church and cemetery.

> 'We met Lieutenant Colonel Buell and proceeded to the middle of the town. On reaching the main street, we went right along to the church passing by the station and through D Company. We met two troops of tanks at the church and had our three-inch mortar sections with us. Sergeant

Military police of 103 Beach Group search German prisoners of war.

Over a hundred of the drowned tanks were recovered and repaired within days.

Drapeau was in charge. The anti-tank guns soon joined us and I had to stop
Sergeant Fitzgerald's boys from firing at the water tower.'

Having cleared through the village and reached the open country inland from the village, after some considerable delays, Lieutenant Colonel Buell reorganized the North Shores before leading them on towards objective Elm. (See Chapter 5).

The Landing of 48 Commando RM

Number 48 Commando was born out of 7 Royal Marine Battalion in March 1944, at the Royal Marine Barracks Deal in Kent. As an OVERLORD priority, Lieutenant Colonel Moulton took his new 'Commando' north to the Commando Training Centre at Achnacarry for an abbreviated conversion and training package. After six gruelling weeks in the Highlands, 48 returned south to the Commando assembly area on the banks of the River Hamble, near Southampton. On 3 June they embarked at Warsash into the ships of Assault Group J4. The commando units assigned to Juno Beach crossed the Channel in the SS *Princess Margaret* and HMS *Prince Albert* and were to be delivered to the beaches by the landing craft of 503rd and 523rd Assault Flotillas.

Lieutenant Colonel Moulton outlined the plan that had been developed by I Corps and Brigadier 'Jumbo' Leicester of 4 Special Service Brigade:

'Between the Canadian 3rd Division on Juno Beach and the British 3rd Division on Sword Beach, there was a gap of five miles, caused by a reef off the coast which prevented landings; No. 48 Commando was immediately behind the North Shore Regiment, the left battalion of the Canadians, wheel left, and clear the beach defences opposite the reef – until it met No. 41 Commando, who would be doing the same thing, coming the other way, after landing behind the right battalion of the British 3rd Division. We were to meet at a group of houses on the stream, which runs through a village, engagingly called Petit Enfer [Luc-sur-Mer]. ... When we started off on our task, a squadron of light support craft would work along the shore to support us.

'... As we should not be under fire when we landed, and as our transport would not be available for the first day, we would land carrying a fairly heavy load of ammunition and explosives. We would dump this at St Aubin and then lightly equipped, would move down a road parallel to the shore to Lagrune. This would be our firm base, and from it we would tackle the coast defences from the rear.'

However, the elegant simplicity of this plan, in common with many D Day plans, did not survive contact with the enemy. The Royal Marines were to be committed to a difficult and bloody fight that tested to the limits the results of their six weeks of commando training in Scotland.

The Canadian official historian recorded that 'An especially unlucky

An LCI (Small) made an unsteady platform from which to disembark.

Commandos landing from their LCIs. Note the mini motorcycle.

Wreckage on the beach at the point wherre 48 Commando landed.

landing was experienced by 48 Commando'. The RM Commando D Day report goes on to explain that:

'Even before touching down on Nan Red beach in six LCI(Small) at H plus 45 minutes, these troops were engaged by machine gun and mortar fire from the beach defenders, who chose at this moment to return to life. They had previously been subdued by the neutralizing fire from sea. The Commando therefore suffered heavy casualties before reaching the beach.'

Colonel Moulton described his unit's run in to the smoke shrouded beach, which at first was relatively uneventful:

'As we closed the beach ... I tried to pick up the beach signs and beach parties. The beach seemed confused and they were difficult to spot, but it was clear that there were a lot of people there, and we could see some signs of work on the beach exit to the right of the houses. Now we were very close. No one seemed to be shooting at us. It was probably all right. Our motion checked sharply and ... we hung rolling on the beach obstacle we had fouled; then a wave caught our stern, swung us, and carried us forward to the beach at a bad angle and rolling. As we struck the obstacle, the enemy opened fire with mortars and machine guns from the esplanade, a little more than a hundred yards away. The sailors replied with crashing bursts of Oerlikon fire.

'I looked around and saw the other landing craft of the squadron in confusion. Our craft and the three next to it on our left had got through to beach reasonably close in, further left the other two were hung up on beach obstacles, helpless and well out from the beach, in the noise and confusion, I realized that the enemy were firing at us and that men were being hit. No question now of our smoke upsetting the Canadians' battle or interfering with the work on the beach – that had all too clearly gone very wrong – and I looked for the mortar men to fire the smoke. Thinking that they would not

be wanted when we were first fired at on the way in, they had dismounted their mortars and gone forward ready to land. I shouted to them, realized that my voice was powerless against the noise, I jumped down from the bridge on the port side and ran forward a few paces to grab one of them by the arm. He looked around, saw me, said something I could not hear, then ran hack to the sandbags and started to mount his [2-inch] mortar. Someone had done the same on the starboard side. Back on the bridge, I realized with a sinking heart that the Commando was meeting something like disaster. Then the mortars popped, and seconds later, hissing out of the sky on to the esplanade to windward, came the blessed smoke bombs. The other craft, seeing our smoke, joined in with theirs, and in a minute or two we were in dense white smoke, and the Germans were firing blind.'

Despite the smoke, some of the wooden LCI, including those of Z Troop, were hit by enemy fire from WN 27 and with little to protect the closely packed troops, casualties were suffered. 48 Commando had expected to make an orderly landing on Nan, with the German defences having already been taken by the Canadians. This was all to evidently not the case. The beach obstacles were still in place and the expected signs, tapes, beach masters and military policemen were not to be seen. Chaos reigned on the beach. Most of the commandos were landed in about three feet of water but, according to 4 Special Service Brigade's war diary, with some of their craft stuck on obstacles:

'Y and Z Troops could only get ashore by swimming. Many heavily laden officers and men attempted to swim ashore from these craft and a high proportion of these were lost, drowning in a strong undertow.

'On reaching shore, troops made for the cover of the earth cliff and sea wall. Here they found a confused situation. The cliff and sea wall gave some protection from SA fire but any movement away from them was under MG fire. The whole area was under heavy mortar and shellfire. Under the sea wall was a jumble of men from other units including many wounded and dead. The beach was congested with tanks, SP guns and other vehicles, some out of action, others attempting to move from the beaches in the very confined space between the water's edge and the sea wall. LCTs were arriving all the time and attempting to land their loads, adding to the general confusion. A quick recce showed that the beach exit to the right of the isolated houses was free from SA fire, except for occasional shots, and that a gap had been cleared through the mines.'

48 landed at 0843 hours, some twenty minutes behind the second wave of the North Shore Regiment. However, as explained, the Canadian infantry had found it an exceedingly slow and costly business to break into WN 27. Colonel Moulton wrote that:

'The time allowed for the Canadians was very short, and in the circumstances quite impossible. We realized this from the start and never *had any inclination to blame the Canadians for our bitter medicine.'*

Colonel Moulton had been hit near the beach by splinters from a mortar bomb but he remained in command despite the pain and discomfort of his wound.

Having crossed the sea wall and made their way through the coastal minefield, leading elements of 48 Commando headed inland to their assembly area. Here, behind the 'crust' of German defences, it was 'much quieter' but Colonel Moulton found that much of his unit was missing. Various estimates have been made as to 48's losses but it is clear that, initially, the Commando mustered only about fifty percent of its strength and that many men had lost equipment, weapons and ammunition, particularly support weapons. Leaving the troops to reorganize in the assembly area, the Colonel retraced his steps back to the beach. Here, according to the war diary:

'A considerable number of men of mixed troops were found under the cliff and these were moved off to the right. He found Y Troop attempting to get ashore from an LCT to which they had transferred from their LCI. However, the landing of Y Troop was very slow and few men managed to get ashore before the LCT shoved off, taking with her about fifty men of the Commando to England despite their energetic protests. Z Troop was more fortunate and about forty men were eventually collected in the assembly area.'

The Colonel collected his men from the beach and led them inland.

With a much-reduced strength but as planned, 48 Commando moved east through the country to the rear of St Aubin towards Sword Beach. After the noise, death and confusion of the beaches, once through the crust of defences, it seemed ominously quiet.

Lagrune-sur-Mer

Having assembled his Commando, Lieutenant Colonel Moulton directed A Troop across the half mile of relatively open country that separated St Aubin and Lagrune. Taking an inland route, their mission was to head towards the farm that had been selected as the Commando's firm base for the clearance operations. Meanwhile, B Troop was moving to clear the sea front houses between the two villages. Having established his headquarters Colonel Moulton:

'...ordered Z Troop to organize its defence and N Troop to start on their sector of house clearing. At some time about then, I sent an officer's patrol to our junction point with No. 41 (RM) Commando.

'Apart from this, B and N Troops had met nothing but snipers and patrols, which withdrew before their advance; a little later, B Troop rejoined us at the farm... X Troop reported that it was held up. Moving along the sea front, they had reached the west side of Lagrune, but could make no further progress. I pressed him for more definite information about what was holding him up, but all he could say was that he was losing a lot of men to snipers. Feeling rather futile, I told ... B Troop to work down the road leading to the seafront on the east side of the village, so getting behind whatever was holding up N Troop. I gave him our one mortar under Lieutenant Mike Aldworth of S [Support] Troop, who had now reached us from the beach, in case he met opposition.

'Soon, B Company reported that they were in contact with the enemy, ... I went down to have a look. We walked through the back gardens, scrambling over walls and pushing our way through side doors; passed Aldworth who started to range his mortar, and came up with the men of B Troop. They were having a good many casualties from light mortar fire, we could see the tails of the bombs flying about, and I told them to keep inside the houses until they were wanted. At last, we reached a house ..., and were directed upstairs to find the OC B Company in the loft. I started to haul myself up through the hatch, but my arm and shoulder felt very sore from mortar bomb splinters, so I stood with my head and shoulders in the hatch, talking to the OC. He said he could see right into a German post, and was quite confident he could capture it as soon as he had a fire plan arranged.

The 'strong point' (WN 26) defended by a reinforced platoon from 9 Kompanie 736 Grenadiers, was centred on a group of fortified houses on Lagrune's sea front and a newly casemated 50mm. The attack on it began with the already below strength B Troop dashing across the lateral road to

In the centre of the town the houses and streets were an integral part of the strong point.

attempt to break into the houses on the far side of the crossroads. However, the Germans had prepared the buildings for defence and according to Colonel Moulton,

> 'They seemed unable to get in. I watched them crouch under the ten-foot wall that blocked the street, and saw half a dozen stick grenades come over it to fall among them. Miraculously, it seemed, there were no casualties.'

Despite the confidence of the company commander, the attack by B Troop had been halted.

The attack on WN 26 was renewed, this time supported by pair of Centaur tanks and a Royal Marine Assault Regiment but this

A Royal Marine Centaur tank with a 9 howitzer. This example is to be found La Breche.

Centaur in action in support of 48 Commando at Lagrune-sur-Mer on the afternoon of D Day.

too failed. The Centaurs' main role had been to bridge the fire support time gap between the end of the amphibious bombardment and the deployment of the SP field artillery ashore. However, the Royal Marine gun crews had belatedly been given Royal Armoured Corps drivers and a mobile role, 'within a mile of the beaches'. However, their landing craft were top heavy and of the eighty Centaurs, only forty-eight made it to shore on the morning of D Day. Most, as planned, remained in the immediate beach area. In the attack on the Lagrune strong point, the first Centaur attempted to destroy an anti-tank wall some six feet high by four feet thick. It used up all its ammunition without seriously damaging the wall, exposing the limitations of the 95mm high explosive. However, the wall would have even challenged the AVRE's Petard demolition gun. The second Centaur ran over a mine amongst the rubble surrounding the defences. Despite the failure to breach the concrete wall, some of the commandos had forced an entry into the strong point but had 'fallen foul of anti-personnel mines'. Colonel Moulton admits that he '... should have had more men close up, ready to back up their momentary success'. He continued his account:

'We were nearly back where we had started, one Centaur less, and the road blocked to tanks. Worse, we now knew that the enemy had built and wired themselves into the block of houses they were holding. It seemed that, until we could knock something down, it was physically impossible to enter, while, by demolishing a house on our side of the crossroads, they had given themselves a clear field of fire to prevent our close approach. While I was

digesting these unpleasant facts, Jumbo Leicester came up and told me to call off further attempts on what we now began to call the Lagrune strong point, and to organise the rest of the village for defence; German armour was moving up towards the coast, and Lagrune was on its axis.'

As darkness fell, the officers' patrol returned from the junction point, reporting that it had seen nothing of 41 Commando but had met no enemy either. Isolated, the commandos prepared their defences and went into their night-time routine. Overnight, Colonel Moulton considered the problem posed by WN 26. How were they going to force an entrance?

'The Germans had so arranged things that they could shoot at us while we were doing so, it was not going to be simple for us, and could be very costly'.

With an uncertain situation inland, the commandos were a low priority for support. However, 21st Panzer Division did not, as expected, push home their attack at dawn and therefore:

'The Brigadier came up and confirmed that ... our job was to finish off the strong point. I realised our duty, both to the military world at large and to our own self-respect, to capture it ourselves and not to leave it to someone else; it would make a great deal of difference to the Commando's future morale to finish the job – and we all, by now, had a personal score to settle. But then weakness: the strong point was beginning to seem impregnable; and it would be nice to stop and lick our wounds, without the prospect of more casualties, more danger and perhaps another failure. Jumbo Leicester's matter-of-fact order was just what I needed, and I recognised not only its

A Canadian M10, Tank Destroyer, moves down the road towards the knocked out Centaur and WN 26.

Dawn 7 June, the strong point is battered by anti-tank gun fire from a M10.

correctness, but the moral stiffening, which I needed, and which it gave me. I tried not to show all this, as I acknowledged his order in what I hoped was an imperturbable way.

'The Brigadier also gave me some tanks to replace the Centaurs: two Canadian M10s and a troop commander's Sherman from the Royal Marine Armoured Support Regiment.'

However, the knocked out Centaur was blocking the route from the lateral road up to the strong point and the open, fire covered, approaches were mined. Amongst the ammunition that the commandos had safely landed were some Bangalore Torpedoes. These were essentially six foot long steel pipes packed with explosives, which when detonated would shred barbed wire defences through which they had been placed. They also caused sympathetic detonations to mines that laid near the torpedoes. Having screwed several Bangalores together end to end, the Commandos used this effect to breach the minefield. Colonel Moulton described the operation:

'We used some smoke; Lieutenant Mackenzie, with some of A Troop, rushed across the road behind the Centaur and into the field, placed the Bangalore Torpedo, checked its placing and lit its fuze, then rushed back into the cover of the houses, and the Bangalore exploded with an almighty hang.

'Covered against possible anti-tank weapons by our men in the houses, one of the M10s went forward, swung clear of the Centaur, followed the line of the Bangalore past it, then swung back into the road. I watched, heart in

German Grenadiers killed during the fighting with 48 Commando.

Commandos inspect the newly
constructed 50mm gun casemate
at Lagrune after the battle.

mouth, fearing to see another mine go up under it; but nothing happened, and now it could blow us a hole in the masonry, it started to fire at the wall across the street. Yesterday, the Centaurs high-explosive shells had burst on the thick, concrete wall and hardly dented it; now, the M10s solid, high-velocity anti-tank projectiles went right through it.'

The M10 used most of its ammunition up but the wall had plenty of small holes in it and one of the Royal Marines' Sherman command tanks was brought up 'to have a go with high-explosive. ... In a while, the wall and the house on one side of it began to crumble'. According to the Royal Marines' D Day report: 'An assault party then went in and seized the houses on either side of the gap. One of these was blown up by a demolition party and the resultant rubble used to fill in the anti-tank ditch inside the wall.' Colonel Moulton continued his account of the end of the battle:

'After a bit, I judged we could make it and gave the word, Lieutenant Mackenzie led the way with A Troop, and I followed with B, then ... X Troop and a working party from Headquarters with shovels and explosives. While A and B Troops worked through the houses along the sea-front, the working party blew down what was left of the wall, and shovelled the debris into the trenches and fire positions around it, so that a tank could pass. Germans were firing down the open promenade, but Mac seemed to be getting along well through the houses. The Sherman ground its noisy way across the debris of the wall onto the promenade, slewed to fire along it, and as it did so put a track into a trench on the promenade and wrenched it off. Hell! Were we going to fail now? The tilted Sherman fired as well as it could down the promenade, and I tried to follow Mac down the houses to see if I could do anything to help him. Then, suddenly, grey figures began to emerge with their hands up. RSM Travers fell them in and checked to see that they were unarmed, and the officer in charge was brought to me, but we had no language in common. As we looked at each other, I saw one of 48 kick a German bottom, and shouted to him to shut up being a fool. Mac came along and reported no further opposition; the prisoners were marched off; and that was that.'

Meanwhile, 41 Commando, who had been landed on Sword Beach, had been attempting to fight westward through the coastal villages of Lion and Luc-sur-Mer to meet up with 48 Commando and link the two beachheads. 41 found the strong point in Lion strongly held and it was only finally overcome on 8 June. Meanwhile, 46 Commando Royal Marines, who had been kept afloat as 4 Special Service Brigade's reserve, were landed and

Prisoners marching to capivity from the Lagrune strong point.

effected the link up on the coast by clearing a strong point at Petit Enfer. The Royal Marine Commandos had been committed to fighting along the coastline, with little support, while I Corps' main effort lay in getting as far inland as possible. The result, as we have seen, was some serious fighting by groups of equally determined men.

Chapter 7

The Douvres Radar Station

The British developed the Chain Home Radar (Radio Direction and Ranging) network in time to make a significant contribution to the victory in the skies over Southern England in 1940. However, the Germans had been independently developing their own version of radio wave technology, which famously included the direction finding equipment for their bombers and by 1941, the Germans were deploying radar along the Channel coast. The technological battle led to Britain's first airborne raid at Bruneval in February 1942. At this site on the coast, east of le Havre, an RAF technician dropped in with 2 Para to seize German radar components. Little did Flight Sergeant Cox know that the Paras were under orders to kill him if he was in danger of falling into enemy hands! Such was the value of the secret radar technology.

By 1944, the *Luftwaffe* had deployed a dense pattern of radar sites (the *Kammhuber* Line) designed to 'vector' night fighter aircraft against British bombers that now were ranging across mainland Europe. German radar provided considerable help in ensuring that night bombing raids could only be carried out at a tremendous cost in both men and aircraft. In the strategic bombing campaign the *per capita* casualties suffered by Bomber Command aircrew almost equalled that of the infantry fighting in the North-West European campaign.

The Douvres-la-Délivrande radar site, manned by 8 *Kompanie* 53 *Luftnachrichten* (Air Signals) Regiment, had become fully operational in August 1943. The four radars were located in two linked sites, in what was to become 3rd Canadian Division's D Day beachhead. In the smaller, northern, site a single *Wasserman* (Allied code name 'Chimney') long-range early warning radar, was surrounded by mines and wire and was defended by *Luftwaffe* personnel manning trenches, 20mm guns and twin *Spandaus* in concrete *Tobruks*. A short distance south across the Beny-Douvres road was a larger site containing two *Freyer* radar, for general air defence, including the direction of anti-aircraft fire, and a single, shorter range (forty miles) but more accurate Giant *Wurzburg* radar that was capable of directing night fighters to individual targets. Five 50mm anti-tank guns, a 75mm field

Freyer radar antenna.

An oblique photograph taken before D Day showing the tall *Freyer* antenna and the smaller *Würtzburg* dish.

gun, and mortars, defended the main site, along with dual purpose ground/anti-aircraft machine guns in bunkers, *Tobruks* and open emplacements. The Douvres site was well constructed with heavy concrete casemates, some of which extended four stories below ground, which sheltered most of the equipment and 200 men. The position was proof against the heaviest bombardment but, while the men and equipment were safe, the radar antennas were in the open, vulnerable to Allied attack.

As the German coastal radar sites could provide timely information that would deny the Allies vital tactical surprise on D Day, the *Kammhuber* Line posed a significant threat to Operation OVERLORD. Consequently, most radar sites were hit during precision attacks by fighter-bombers. Those that were left operational were used in the D Day deception plan, which included exploitation of the electromagnetic spectrum, by the use of strips of radar reflecting metal foil, code named 'Window'. These metal strips were dropped by aircraft to distract the Germans by producing the electronic signature of a mass attack at the Pas de Calais. Douvres, along with all other sites in Normandy received the constant attention of the Allied air forces. However, despite this attention, the Douvres radar antennas were active to some extent until the Germans destroyed the sets just before they were captured on D+11.

The village of Douvres-la-Délivrande and the radar site were towards the left flank of the 3rd Canadian Division's D Day area. 8 Cdn Brigade were scheduled to capture the site with the support of 30 Commando's technical specialists, whose task was to secure items of intelligence interest such as radar equipment. As has already been mentioned, the North Shores had been held up by stronger opposition than anticipated at the village of Tailleville. Consequently, 8 Brigade ordered the radar site to be by-passed and the Queen's Own and the Chaudiere were to continue their advance inland on a more westerly route via Beny-sur-Mer,

> '...after which 9 Cdn Brigade could be passed through on its axis towards Carpiquet. The North Shores were now being left behind and Tailleville was only occupied during the course of the evening. Here the Battalion were to reorganize overnight after twelve hours in action and very little sleep during the previous thirty-six hours.'

General Keller's orders for the night 6-7 June and the following day were sent out by dispatch rider at 2115 hours. 8 Cdn Brigade were 'to contain Douvres-la-Délivrande with a view to clearing it at first light in the morning'.

The First Attack

On the morning of 7 June the North Shore resumed their advance in a southerly direction from Tailleville and they promptly bumped into an enemy position in the woods south-west of the village. A Company, as recorded in the war diary, overcame enemy resistance, 'With the co-operation of the tanks, the position was taken and two officers and thirty six other ranks were taken prisoner of war'. The war diarist goes on to recount a bitty and frustratingly slow advance to their objective, the radar station.

> 'Considerable sniping in Tailleville and forward of A Company is very

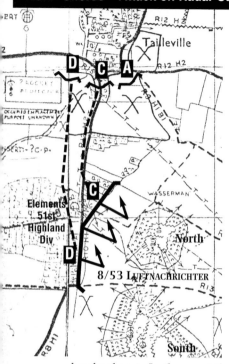

annoying and slowing up the advance. Progress is slow and the ammunition dump in the woods blew up, which temporarily halted the advance.

'*C Company who had been sweeping the woods and scrub on the left, moved over and cleared through the HQ dug-out in the Wood* [Alternative HQ II/736 Grenadiers]. *Only four prisoners of war were taken from this area but it was found later that they had escaped to the rear and surrendered to 9 Cdn Brigade's HQ. This HQ position was well dug in with underground offices, trenches, cookhouse and so on.*'

In this position, C Company reorganized for the attack on the radar station.

I Corp's intelligence estimate prior to D Day was that the *Luftwaffe* specialists would not have the stomach for a fight and that the site as a whole would have been severely damaged by the bombardment. In the event the Intelligence officers were proved to be wrong on both counts.

The North Shores had a squadron of the Fort Garry Horse's Shermans under command and, in support, the thirty-two 25-pounders of 19 Cdn Field Regiment, which complimented its own machine guns, mortars and anti-tank guns. However, Lieutenant Day complained, with justification, that

'*... the central area of the objective was huge and we were not permitted to bring fire down on the central sector for fear of destroying the radar equipment which the Commandos particularly wanted to capture intact.*'

With restricted fire support, C Company attacked the radar site but, according to the official historian, they 'produced little results and eventually even a battalion effort met with no more success'. An entry in the North Shore's war diary summarized the situation.

'*The Radar Station was found to be stronger than had been anticipated and was engaged by 19 Cdn Fd Regt, which was in support of us. Our mortars also took on the Station but as the concrete works were rather thick and well dug-in, little or no damage was done. The day was fast drawing to a close and a decision was finally made and Bde permission obtained to by-pass the Station and move on to the Bde RV.*'

The Douvres position was the only significant part of their intermediate D

Northern Site

Douvres →

Minefield
boundaries

← Beny

Southern Site

A replacement *Würtzburg* dish and control cabin at Douvres. This dish had been used by the French in post-war radar experiments.

The shorter range and more accurate *Würtzburg* was used to vector night fighters to their target.

Day objective (Line Elm) that the Canadians were unable to take. To release the Canadians to move inland, 51st Highland Division, I Corps' follow up infantry formation, were tasked to deal with the radar site.

Lieutenant Colonel Thompson's orders were to take 5 Black Watch forward to the radar station but he set off with scant information other than 'there were a pocket of Germans holding out' and the limited detail he could glean from the overprinted intelligence map. 5 Black Watch were allocated two AVREs to help deal with the concrete defences. As the Scottish infantry moved forward, they were assured that the Canadians had moved on inland. Their route to the radar station took them through a wood:

> *'It was very thick and movement very difficult in it. Troops were encountered, who were taken for Germans. They were in fact Canadians. But after that little trouble had been sorted out, Thompson got ahead. There was a wide open space beyond the wood and between it and the radar station. This was being swept by a murderous enemy fire, and it was evident that the station was much more strongly held than had been supposed. An 88mm gun, firing somewhere from Douvres village itself, accounted for the two RE vehicles.'*

It was clear that the Black Watch would need greater support but Lieutenant Colonel Thompson was ordered to disengage his battalion and pull back 'although he planned a new form of attack from the rear of the objective, orders came that he was to by-pass the radar station, which was left to be shelled by the Navy'. *Oberleutenant* Ingle and 238 men of 8 *Kompanie* 53 *Luftnachrichten* Regiment were to hold out and provide a valuable observation and reporting service. The garrison was made up of about 160 *Luftwaffe* technicians and a mixed bag of soldiers from 716 Division who had been ousted from their own positions on the beaches earlier in the day. Eventually, 4 Special Service Brigade took over the task of containing the enemy in the radar site. 48 Commando and 46 Commando, initially, took over the responsibility but on 10 June, the radar site and the positions surrounding it came under control of 41 Commando.

During this period, the Douvres radar site was considered to be 'More of a hindrance than a nuisance'. However, from the casemates, the Germans could not only operate some of their radar but they could also pass back information on Allied activities in the centre of Second Army's area, as well as providing target information. The site also represented to the Germans a valuable pivot for the Germans planned attempt to drive the Allies back into the sea. *Oberleutnant* Ingle was exhorted by the surviving telephone line to hold his position. His garrison, secure underground and being within three or four miles of promised relief, had little reason to surrender.

By 11 June, 41 Commando had been left on their own to contain the largely inactive German garrison in their casemates. However, with other Commando units marching to more active parts of the front, 41 Commando's Mortar Platoon were detached as the Germans in the Douvres radar site 'wouldn't have even heard their 3-inch bombs explode'. In order to let the enemy know that they hadn't been forgotten about, they were regularly attacked by rocket firing Typhoons. In addition, two Centaur tanks were placed under command of 41 Commando. The task of these two AFVs was to provide close support and to join in the harassing fire programme that was laid down by the Commando's PIATs, 2-inch mortars, Bren guns and snipers.

> 'This was designed largely to deter movement between their various "safe havens" during the hours of daylight. 'F' Troop came across a German anti-tank gun with a supply of ammunition and were delighted to fire it off at the slightest provocation.'

This harassing fire also prevented the German technicians from coming out of their casemates and repairing cables to the radar antenna. However, in true Commando style, 41 were not content to dominate the ground with fire alone.

> 'Reconnaissance patrols during the hours of darkness were a major factor in keeping up to date with the situation of the surrounded Germans. Of great value in this task were the handful of attached German speaking men of 10 (Inter-Allied) Commando who were at times able to assess conditions in the bunkers by overhearing German conversations. Their

The bombardment prior to the attack on the radar station.

senior rank was CSM O'Neill although he was neither Irish nor even British but a Czechoslovakian by birth who, like all other commandos who had family in their home countries, had adopted an 'English' name for the duration of the war.

A recce patrol on 12 June reported that the northern radar station had been abandoned by the Germans. Therefore, it was decided that, once it was dark, a twenty man fighting patrol provided by A Troop would enter the Northern radar site and 'verify the situation [but] if the station was found to be occupied, it should withdraw'. The patrol was to be supported by six AVREs of 5 Assault Squadron RE. Raymond Mitchell wrote:

'At 0100 hours on 13 June, CSM O'Neill led a party forward to blow a gap in the outer wire using bangalore torpedoes ... By 0200 the AVREs had approached to the northern edge of the minefield and were engaged in hurling their Flying Dustbins at the bunkers: in view of their short range ... they had to get in close. This provoked no response from the enemy, so the patrol moved through the outer wire and Lt Stevens led two men forward to blow the inner wire. On the explosion of the bangalore torpedo, the Germans opened up with MGs and machine-carbines from four separate locations, but were firing very wildly and obviously did not know the exact position of their attackers. A firefight ensued for about fifteen minutes then, as instructed, the patrol withdrew at about 0300 without casualties. For some time thereafter, the Germans vented their spleen by subjecting the Commando positions to heavy shell and mortar fire'.

This proved that the Germans were still in communication with their fellow countrymen whose artillery positions were by now south of the Caen-Bayeux road.

On the night of 14 June, a German aircraft attempted a supply drop to their beleaguered comrades. However, as recorded by the Commando's historian:

'In the event, 'P Troop were quicker off the mark than the Germans and their men reached the containers first. Instead of the food or water, however,

which had been assumed to be the enemy's major requirements, the delivery comprised breech blocks for PAKs, [anti-tank guns] small arms ammunition, booby traps and instruments.'

The commandos continued to penetrate the sites' defences and it is recorded that some patrols:

'... worked their way through the wire and mines right up to the casemates and on one such incursion, Sgt Hazelhurst of 'A' Troop banged on the steel door of one of the bunkers with the butt of his Tommy gun, yelling, "Come out, you silly bastards!" but to no avail.'

The Germans holding out at Douvres were becoming notorious and with numerous reporters now in Normandy, it was only a matter of time before they attracted their attention. BBC reporter Robert Barr recorded a description at the scene at the radar station on the morning of 17 June 1944.

'There is still one German strong point which is holding out within six miles of the Normandy coast and many miles behind our front line. The Navy have had a try at smashing it. The Air Force had a try. But still the German garrison held out. We've called off all big-scale attempts to clear it up because the commander in the area has ruled that no heavy casualties must be risked in smashing it. But the point is that this strong point of the West Wall, which the Canadians swept past in the first day is still intact. All you can see of it is ordinary fields, with a few grass mounds here and there indicating defence points. You can see a concrete tower hidden amongst trees, and through binoculars you can see the signs: "Achtung. Minen". "Beware of mines." This is a sample of what the Germans hoped to prepare for us along the coast. We've surrounded it, we've shelled it, we've bombed it, and it's still unopened.'

The Allies had been happy to simply contain the enemy but, but by 14 June

One of the AVRES knocked out during the battle to clear the radar site.

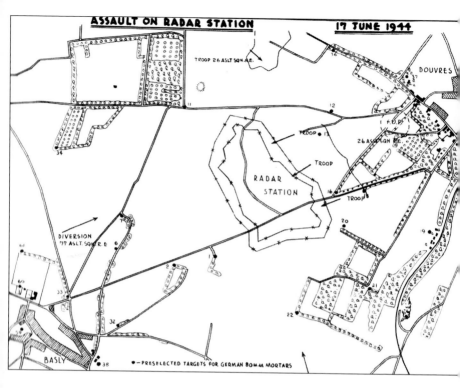

ASSAULT ON RADAR STATION   17 JUNE 1944

DOUVRES

TROOP 26 ASLT SQN. A.E.

RADAR STATION

TROOP

DIVERSION
77 ASLT. SQDN. R. E.

BASLY

●—PRESELECTED TARGETS FOR GERMAN 80M.M MORTARS

the German *Luftwaffe* technicians sheltering in the Douvres radar site were effectively denying a large area of valuable terrain in the restricted beachhead. In particular, the Germans were hindering the use of an airstrip built for RAF Typhoon aircraft, 'whose pilots were not greatly enamoured to have to brave machine gun fire as they took-off and landed!' Finally, 41 Commando's casualties from German fire were mounting and the Royal Marines were ordered to 'Get them out!'

The Capture of the radar site

On 16 June 1944, 41 Commando prepared its plan of attack. Lieutenant Colonel Palmer had assembled forty-four armoured vehicles to assist with the task, including flails of B Squadron 22 Dragoons, reinforced by troops from C Squadron, and four troops of AVREs from 5 Assault Squadron RE. The 7.2-inch guns of a Royal Artillery heavy regiment were to supplement the normal support of the field artillery regiments..

The attack was to be preceded by a thirty minute naval and heavy artillery bombardment. However, as the Royal Marines commented, 'even their 202-pound shells did little more than chip the massive concrete bunkers, and perhaps giving the inmates a slight headache'. Meanwhile the AVREs of 77 Squadron were to mount a noisy and obvious diversionary attack on the main radar site from the south, just before H Hour. The importance of planning input by officers from 79th Armoured Division was now becoming clear as they had quickly learned that:

> '... Crabs or AVREs placed under command of the infantry would be mishandled and suffer heavy casualties. Particularly did they not allow for the short range of the Petard and consequent vulnerability of AVREs.'

The infantry's lack of cross training with 79th Armoured Division's various equipments was telling. There had been too little time in the run up to D Day. Hobart's divisional staff had sought to overcome the technical challenges presented by the coastal defences and the resulting vale of secrecy over their activity was only reluctantly lifted to key personnel. However, after two weeks in action, lessons had been learned and 41's plan, conceived with help of assault engineer officers, was effective in its execution.

The bombardment began at 1630 hours and, as planned at 1700, the armour advanced. Half of B Squadron's Sherman flails, two vehicles each attached to the four troops of AVREs, started to beat their way through the wire and across the minefields surrounding the two radar sites. The remainder of the squadron gave covering fire with particular attention to the five anti-tank guns. The Dragoon's history records that:

A commando inspects the technical equipment in one of the casemates.

'In clouds of dust, and with a shattering clanking of chains, the flails moved into the minefield. German machine guns stuttered away here and there, swishing around them apparently at random. From a patch of dead ground, a group of supporting flails, hull down, loosed off machine guns and 75mm shell to keep the German heads down. For half an hour and more, the flails moved smoothly on, biting through the minefield and touching off mines that sent up tall pillars of heavy black smoke. Then they were through, and in the most leisurely manner the AVREs rolled up the lanes to the mouths of the fortresses, ... But there was little opposition; there could not be, for the whole area was swept by fire from the flails.'

With the enemy subdued, the AVREs drove through the breaches and engaged the casemates with their Petards. Lance Corporal Sorensen, an AVRE driver described how:

'... the [AVRE] Squadron moved up to the forward start line, which was about half a mile from the radar station and concealed from it by trees and a farm. ... At about 1700 hours, we moved forward.

'We penetrated about one-third of the minefield before anything happened. But then we came under heavy anti-tank fire. ...I could see a column of dust and smoke go up as a shell landed and the flashes from the 75mm guns of the Crabs as they replied.

'The AVRE in front of me succeeded in getting its offside track in a deep trench and it was stuck there immovable. My commander gave me the order to overtake on the left. As I did so, there was a terrific concussion and my vehicle gave a lurch. My instrument panel lights went out as well as all the interior lights. My first impression was that we had hit a mine and 1 tried the steering to see if the tracks were intact. As I did so, I saw my co-driver lying with a terrible wound in his head. He was unmistakably dead, and I then realized we had been hit by a shell. The next moment, the whole compartment caught fire. I was almost suffocated by flame, but managed to open the hatch over my head enough to scramble through. As I was climbing out, the ammunition in the hull Besa was exploding and a piece of shrapnel hit me in the right leg. I jumped clear and ran for a bomb crater about fifteen yards away. I was joined by my wireless operator and my gunner. Hardly had we dropped into it when my tank blew up. The force of the explosion blew the turret, which weighs about ten tons, fifty yard away.

'...On my, way back out of the position, I saw the other tank crews place their 70-pound charges on top of the underground emplacements and lie doggo until they were blown. ... The white flag appeared and the job was done.'

The job was not however, completely 'done' until the position had been thoroughly cleared and prisoners rounded up. Following through the three gaps at 1720 hours were B, P and X Troops, while A Troop attacked the smaller northern site. Y Troop remained in reserve. However, by this time, the Commando's war-diarist wrote '...the enemy had been dazed, shocked or frightened into surrender and came out with their hands up.' Once their protective concrete had been breached, the *Luftwaffe* technicians had promptly given up. The battle was over by 1830 hours, with 227 Germans being taken prisoner, including five officers. In 22 Dragoon's history the prisoners were described as, 'for the most part badly shaken and dispirited men, glad to be out of it all'.

41 Commando suffered one casualty during the attacks, while the Dragoons had four Crabs disabled due to mine damaged tracks but all four were repairable. Closing with the enemy, the Royal Engineers lost four AVREs knocked out and three damaged, with three Sappers killed and seven wounded.

The following morning, having just walked around the Radar Site, Frank Gillard returned to the BBC studio five miles away in Chateau Creully and recorded a short report that was broadcast later that day:

'You have heard of that colossal strong-point just along the coast at Douvres where getting on for 200 Germans held out till last night. That's a place to see. Somebody this morning called it an inverted skyscraper. That's not an unreasonable description. Fifty feet and more into the ground it goes – four stories deep. On the surface, you barely notice it. The top's almost flush with the ground. But going down those narrow concrete stairways you think of going into the vaults of the Bank of England. And the Germans did themselves well down below there – central heating, electric light, hot water, air conditioning, radios, telephones, comfortable well-furnished rooms and offices, well-equipped workshops and ample

50mm in an open casemate at Douvres.

Commandos inspect British and German graves. In the background the wrecked *Freyer* radar tower.

supplies of food and ammunition. The Germans who were standing here on this ground fourteen days ago certainly must have thought that they had little to fear, and yet what a change now!

Conclusion

During the afternoon of that same day, Frank Gillard was driven in a Jeep back down to Juno Beach and recorded another report for broadcast by the BBC:

'I'm looking towards the bay now, it is really an almost unbelievable sight. It's stiff with shipping. Warships, landing craft, merchant vessels – everything right down to motor-launches and small boats. There they are, their signal lights winking in the late evening sun, an occasional siren hooting. Overhead, the sky – there's hardly a cloud to be seen anywhere; but the sky's picked out with silver barrage balloons, as thick as currants in a pre-war Christmas cake. And of course we've got our air cover, they're up there now, as they are every moment of the day. And so, on this ground where a fortnight ago the Germans were masters, tonight the Allies are in complete control. I stood by the roadside yesterday and watched the men and machines and supplies rolling in. And a soldier beside me – I don't know who he was – just turned and said: "Once you've seen all this, you know we just can't help winning this war." That's how we all feel here.'

The way into France across Juno Beach had been bought by Canadian blood and heroism.

Chapter 8

A Tour of the Juno Area

The tour described in this chapter starts with some recommended visits to sites associated with Juno Beach on the UK side of the Channel. The Normandy tour will lead the visitor around the scene of the D Day battles fought in the immediate coastal areas and inland from Juno Beach. It is assumed that the visitor will have transport, be it minibus, car or bicycle. However, the distance between Mike Sector and Lagrune-sur-Mer to the west of Courseulles, is short enough for a six-mile round trip walk along the shoreline which takes in most of the D Day sites. Included at the end of the tour is a visit to the Douvres radar site.

HMS *Belfast*.

HMS *Belfast*

The cruiser HMS *Belfast* is to be found moored on the south bank of the River Thames in London, between Tower and London Bridges. The ship carried the flag of Rear Admiral Dalrymple-Hamilton commander of Bombardment Force E and engaged the Ver-sur-Mer Battery and targets in the Juno area throughout 6 June 1944. *Belfast* is a part of the Imperial War Museum and highlights the part played by the Allied Navies on D Day and during the Normandy Campaign. Well worth a visit.

Southwick House

Many of those visiting Normandy and Juno Beach will cross the Channel on ferry services from Portsmouth. In the village of Southwick, just inland from the port is the Royal Naval shore station HMS *Dryad*. Here Admiral Ramsey established his headquarters and was joined by Generals Eisenhower and Montgomery to make the momentous and risky decision to launch D Day on 6 June 1944. Southwick House is now the Wardroom of HMS *Dryad*. However, it is possible, with prior arrangement, to visit the map room, with its wall sized map set up as it was on D Day. An audio commentary describes the use of the house as Admiral Ramsey's HQ, which is complimented by a number of pictures, charts and maps. To book a visit, please ring 02392 284968 (ask for extension 4418)

Portsmouth D Day Museum

Standing on the sea front at Southsea, overlooking the Solent where the fleet of ships carrying 3rd Canadian and 50th British Divisions assembled, the D Day Museum is well worth a visit before heading to the ferry port. Outside the Museum is a Sherman tank painted in the colours of The Fort Garry Horse. Montgomery's statue is on the shoreline nearby.

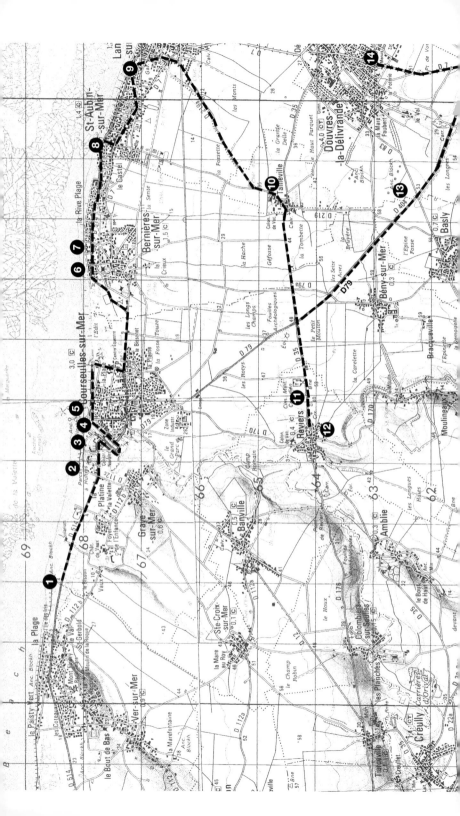

Juno Area

This tour takes the visitor around the scene of the action on the beaches and some of the inland sites. Please be warned that as a battlefield tour, it is not designed to take the visitor to every regimental or liberation memorial which abound in the Juno area.

The tour starts at *Wiederstandnest* 32 at the very western end of Juno Beach. Courseulles is the nearest town and is signposted from Ouisterham, the Caen *Peripherique*, the N13 and from Bayeux. From Arromanches **take the D 514** towards Courseulles, pass through Ver-sur-Mer and after 700 yards **turn left** onto a narrow track marked **Brech le Bisson**. From Courseulles, take the D 514 towards Arromanches. Pass through **two sets** of traffic lights and **after 1,000 yards turn right** onto the *Brech le Bisson* track. There is ample parking a few yards from the casemate.

Wiederstandnest 32

This point is on the right flank of Juno Beach. It is also on the junction with Love Sector of Gold Beach. This strong point was held by a platoon of German infantry, principally to protect the unusual double anti-tank casemate. Sited on the crest of the dunes, the strong point was well hit by naval gunfire and the casemate bears the mark of a strike from a heavy naval shell. Consequently this small position did not resist C Company, The Canadian Scottish, for long and the anti-tank casemate was, reputedly, out of action by the time the infantry approached.

Looking east along Mike Beach to the next *Wiederstandnest* (31) at the base of the Cross of Lorraine 1,800 yards away, is a 75mm that covered the same stretch of beach i.e. overlapping arcs of fire. Beyond *Wiederstandneste* 31 is the town of Courseulles and the village of Bernières. Note two of the many church spires that made life so difficult for landing craft to identify their correct beach.

Driving towards Courseulles on the D 514, the turning to the municipal campsite 'Camping Canadian Scottish' is the road leading from Mike 1 Gap. Alongside the traffic lights, is a stone memorial to the Inns of Court Yeomanry, I Corps' recce regiment. A Squadron landed on Mike Beach during the early afternoon and using this route off the beach set out on their abortive mission to the Odon and Orne River crossings some thirteen miles inland. Continue on to the next traffic lights.

Gap Mike 2 ❷

At the traffic light, **turn left** on to **Avenue General De Gaulle**, towards the dunes and the large steel cross. Park near the AVRE 'One Charlie'. This is the Winnipeg Rifles' Mike Red Beach. A Company were first ashore, landing in this area. To avoid casualties the infantry were to have landed behind the DD tanks and the assault armour but in the event landed ahead of both! When they eventually arrived the 'funnies' of Number 1 and 2 Troops, 26 Assault Squadron RE, created Number Two Gap, which lies behind 'One Charlie' and is still used today. This vehicle is the best example of a restored AVRE to be found on the invasion coast. Heading east along the beach several large casemates of the western part of *Wiederstandnest* 31 can be found amongst the dunes. The first is a 75 mm casemate just beyond the lifeguard station. Further along the dunes, built for a 50 mm, another casemate is located by the sailing club building. Other parts of the smaller concrete structures can be seen protruding from the dunes. B Company, The Winnipeg Rifles fought most of the day to clear this extensive *Wiederstandneste*.

The large Cross of Lorraine commemorates General De Gaulle's return to France on 14 June. He visited Montgomery at his headquarters at Creully before going on to Bayeux, where he was photographed surrounded by enquiring locals wondering who was the tall man with the big nose. Also landing nearby were Prime Minister Winston Churchill on 12 June and King George VI on 16 June. The NTL totem describes how a group of *Osttruppen* held out until D+1 in a solarium in this area.

Wiederstandneste 31 (Courseulles West) and Museum ❸

Continue along the concrete road past the Sailing Club to the Juno Beach Centre and park. The new museum opened on 6 June 2003 stands in the eastern part of the extensive *Wiederstandneste* 31. In front of the Museum is a command post bunker, the large steel ring is all that remains of an observation post cupola. Further right is the remains of the only 88mm casemates to be found in the Juno area. It covers the entrance to Courseulles harbour and Mike Green Beach.

The Museum not only covers the operations on Juno Beach but the part played by the Canadians in general during the war. This modern Museum, largely manned by Canadian students is well worth a visit. Entrance fee payable.

Courseulles East ❹

Either walk from the Museum into the town via the footbridge or drive into Courseulles and park by the aquarium. A 50mm KW39 gun, originally set in an octagonal weapons pit, remains covering the inner approaches to the port's inner basin. The shield of this obsolescent tank gun bears some impressive scars inflicted by direct Allied fire. Across the road is the Canadian DD tank 'Bold' that belonged to B Squadron 1st Hussars. This tank was recovered from the seabed after twenty-seven years and restored to a high standard. While the propellers of the DD conversion kit are missing, the gears that drove them can be seen. The tank bears small memorials to units that landed on this part of Juno Beach. Included are the crests of HMCS *Algonquin* and *Souix*.

Wiederstandneste 29 – Couseulles ❺

A hundred yards further east is a large wooden dagger monument to the Winnipeg Rifles despite the fact that this was the area assaulted by the Regina Rifles. Post-war development and realignment of the sea wall has removed virtually every trace of WN

Combined Operations officers examine the Courseulles defences. The dismounted tank gun covered the dockside at Courseulles then and now.

29. It has completely disappeared and the area is now occupied by the municipal swimming pool and blocks of holiday flats.

Continue east along **Avenue de la Combattante** to the T-Junction and turn right at the traffic lights filter left back on to the D 514 towards Bernières. Do not follow the signs into Bernières but follow the road around to the left. After half a mile, when the road is again running parallel to the coast, park in the car park near the Comitee du Debarquement monument.

The D Day Buildings – Bernières

This area was much photographed on D Day, not least because this was the point that Major General Keller landed. Some time can be spent making 'then and now' comparisons with the buildings on the beach and the old railway station building just inland.

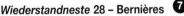

Wiederstandneste 28 – Bernières ⑦

Either walk along the coastal walk or drive 100 yards and park on the wide verge opposite the *Intermarche* **supermarket**. Walk down to the casemate and the beach huts. This 50mm anti-tank gun casemate is again much photographed and is today

Memorial plaque Bernières

surrounded by Canadian war memorials and those belonging to other units who landed in this sector, including the Hackney Battalion of the Royal Berkshire Regiment, who worked with the Beach Group. The level of the beach is higher than in 1944 but the upper part of the old curved seawall can be seen along with a small solid anti-tank round embedded in the seaward side of the 50mm casemate.

Follow the D514 east. After half a mile, at a junction with large flowerbeds where the road changes into the **D7** and heads inland, turn left on the **D514** sign posted to **St Aubin la Plage**. A short way down the road is a left turning into **Avenue des Hirrondelles**, where the house **6** that features in one of the much shown D Day film sequences can be found.

Wiederstandneste 27 – St Aubin **8**

The location of this strong point is easily identified by the 50mm anti-tank gun casemate and a sizeable group of flags and memorials on the seafront, chief amongst which are the North Shore's and the Fort Garry Horse's memorials. Parking is normally available in this area. This is the only casemate of this design complete with gun that is left on the invasion front. The majority of the strong point has been lost to coastal erosion or lies under the car park and cliff area to the left of the memorial.

Follow the one way system from the seafront, turning left onto **Rue Maraechal Foch** and following the road past the crucifix to the roundabout. Follow the sign to Lagune-sur-Mer Plage on **Avenue Marseret**. After 400 yards turn left at the halt sign onto **Boulevarde Maritime**. Turn right and head into Lagrune's seafront square and park.

Wiederstandneste 26 – Lagrune-sur-Mer **9**

The strong point, based on a 50mm anti-tank gun and several *Tobruk* machine gun positions, was one of the smaller coastal defensive positions, as the bluffs flanking Lagrune made this an unlikely spot for a major landing. There is little to be seen of the

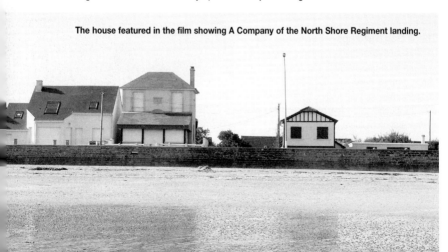

The house featured in the film showing A Company of the North Shore Regiment landing.

German defences except for the rebuilt houses at the rear of the square. The square contains an NTL totem, a US Army truck crushed into a cube to represent the destruction of war and, more conventionally, a memorial to 48 Commando Royal Marines.

The route out of Lagrune to Taillerville is by minor unsigned roads. Retrace your steps back towards St Aubin. Turn left onto **Route Mal. Montgomery** – an insubstantial street. At the crossroads by the Hotel Restaurant de la Mer take **Voie 48 Commando**. This is the area that the Commandos spent the night of 6/7 June before renewing their attack. Turn right at the tennis courts onto **Route de Taillerville (D219a)**. Driving across the open country it is easy to appreciate the open fields of the field of fire enjoyed by the German anti-tank and machine gunners as the Canadians debauched from the coastal towns.

Tailleville 🔟

Tailleville is a good example of the inland villages, which normally consist of a chateau, large farmhouses, agricultural buildings and more modest dwellings. All are substantial constructions built from local stone. The concrete *Tobruk* machine gun position, now converted to a flowerbed, and the roof of a troop shelter can be seen by the entrance to a farm on the second bend on the way into the village. Look out for the Juno Committee marker. Continue west through the village along the D35 signposted to **Reviers** and **Bayeux**. The first cross roads (D79a) was the axis of the inland advance of the Queen's Own Rifles of Canada and the Chaudiere. There was an extensive company defensive position dug in the fields to your right. Continue across the main D79 for a further 1,000 yards and park by the Canadian Cemetery.

CWGC Canadian Cemetery Bény-sur-Mer/Reviers 1️⃣1️⃣

This cemetery, containing 2,049 graves, of which all but five are Canadian, is located on the D35 in the open country east of the village of Reviers. 3rd Canadian Division's machine gun battalion, The Cameron Highlanders of Ottawa, has a memorial plaque located in the left hand of the two observation towers. The graves in the cemetery are

Bény-sur-Mer CWGC Cemetery.

The Giant Wurzburg Radar Dish at the southern site.

mainly but by no means exclusively, post-war concentration from the fighting between D Day and the middle of July. It is a particularly moving place for Canadians to visit and comments in the visitors' book from US visitors often underline how little known is the part played by their fellow North Americans.

Revieres ⑫

Little evidence of the fighting is to be found in this village with its bridge over the small River Mue and the bridge a little further on over the river Seulles. However, there is a small memorial in the village to the Queen's Own Rifles of Canada at the centre of the village.

Retrace the route back past the Canadian Cemetery and turn right onto the **D 79** towards Douvers la Delivrande. Look out for the signs for **Musee Radar.**

The Douvres-la-Delivrande Radar Site ⑬

This fenced site, run by the Caen Memorial, is normally only open during July and August. However, it has been known to open for groups outside these dates. It is always worth checking opening hours with the Radar Museum (Tel: 02 31 06 06 43) or via the Memorial (Tel: 02 31 96 66 05). Even without the site being open, enough can be seen of the enemy positions and the surrounding area to appreciate the problems experienced by the North Shores, the Black Watch, 41 Commando and their supporters. The large dish of a Giant Würtzburg radar can easily be seen. If the site is open, the massive casemates make a very informative visit. The radar technology used by the Germans and how the Allies overcame it to achieve tactical surprise, is explained in a simple but engaging manner. There is an entrance fee. The equally massive bunkers of the northern site are not fenced and can be seen in the fields to the north but they are difficult to reach.

Return to the **D79** and continue towards Douvres la Deliverande. At the **roundabout** turn on to the **D7** again following the signs to Douvres.

CWGC Cemetery Douvres-la-Delivrande ⑭

This cemetery is located on **D7** in the **southern outskirts** of the town. It contains 1,123 graves, of which, the majority, 927 are British, 11 are Canadians and 180 are German. There is also a grave of an Australian airman who was killed on D Day. Again this is a post-war concentration cemetery and although there is a group of D Day graves including some Canadians, the burials span virtually the whole Normandy campaign.

This concludes the tour. To return to the invasion coast continue north through Douvres la Delivrande following signs towards Lagrune-su-Mer. To reach Caen turn and head south on the D7 to the *Peripherique*. Those heading to Bayeux should drive into Douvres la Delivrande and pick up signs for the city and head west on the D35/D176/D12.

Visits to the Bayeux Area

If time allows, it is worth finishing off the tour with a visit to Bayeux. The city was captured virtually undamaged, against slight opposition, by troops of 50th Division on D+1. Take the ring road to the south of Bayeux. This road was built as a by-pass by the Royal Engineers to take the heavy logistic traffic from Arromanches around the choke points in the narrow streets of the city.

Bayeux Museum

This excellent museum concentrates on the inland battles and the breakout. There is plenty to see including mannequins dressed in a wide range of uniforms, vehicles, weapons, equipment and documents. The thirty-five minute film is shown alternatively in English and French. Outside there are fine examples of a Sherman tank, M10 tank destroyer, a Churchill (Crocodile conversion – without its fuel trailer) and a German assault gun. There are also several memorials to British units in the Museum grounds. Allow at least an hour and a half to make the most of the museum. Entrance fee payable.

CWGC Cemetery Bayeux

Just a little further along the ring road is the largest World War II CWGC cemetery in France, which contains the last resting-place of soldiers from virtually every service, arm, branch and regiment of the British forces who fought in the Normandy campaign. Located on the south-western edge of Bayeux, the cemetery is adjacent to the sector of Second Army's Rear Maintenance Area which, was allocated to the Medical Services. Many of the original burials were soldiers who died of wounds in the nearby field hospitals. However, most of the 4,648 burials are the result of the post war concentration of graves. Of the Bayeux graves, 3,935 are British, 181 are Canadian and of the remainder, there are twenty-five Poles, seventeen Australians, eight New Zealanders, seven Russians, three Frenchmen and two each from Czechoslovakia and Italy. The total is completed by 466 Germans and a single unknown body. The Germans are almost exclusively soldiers who died of wounds having been taken prisoner. The Juno area graves in the cemetery are exclusively British, post-war, concentrations, with bodies having been moved from battlefield cemeteries established behind the dunes by 103 Beach Group. The front row of Plot 14 is almost entirely made up of Royal Marines from 48 Commando who were killed on D Day and moved here from the original Commando Cemetery at Bernières. Opposite them is a group of Royal Engineer graves belonging to men who were killed in action while crewing the 'funnies' of 79th Armoured Division. The men are probably from a single AVRE crew.

Order of Battle 3rd Canadian Division
(Assault Phase Grouping)

HQ 3rd Canadian Division
    3rd Canadian Divisional Signals Regiment

HQ 2nd Canadian Armoured Brigade (Under Command)
    2nd Canadian Armoured Brigade Signal Squadron

HQ 7th Canadian Infantry Brigade (Mike and Nan Green)
    J Section Signals 3rd Canadian Infantry Division
    7th Canadian Infantry Brigade Defence Platoon
    The Royal Winnipeg Rifles
    The Regina Regiment
    1st Canadian Scottish Regiment
    B Squadron, 22nd Dragoons (Two Troops) - Flails
    6th Canadian Armoured Regiment (1st Hussars) – DD Tanks
    54th Canadian Light Aid Detachment (RCEME)
    A & D Coys, Cameron Highlanders of Ottawa (MMG & mor)
    12th Canadian Field Regiment - SP artillery
    13th Canadian Field Regiment - SP artillery
    94th Canadian Anti-tank Battery
    248th Battery, 62nd Anti-Tank Regiment (M10 SP guns)
    246th Battery, 62nd Anti-Tank Regiment (17-pounder guns)
    26th Assault Squadron Royal Engineers - AVRE
    6th Canadian Field Company - Engineers
    5th Canadian Field Company - Engineers
    Canadian Field Ambulance
    36th Canadian Light Aid Detachment (RCEME)
    F Section 9th Canadian Provost Company
    7th Beach Group

HQ 8th Canadian Infantry Brigade (Nan Red and White)
    K Section Signals 3rd Canadian Infantry Division
    8th Canadian Infantry Brigade Defence Platoon
    The Queen's Own Rifles of Canada
    Le Regiment de la Chaudiere
    The North Shore (New Brunswick) Regiment
    10th Canadian Armoured Regiment (Fort Garry's Horse)
    55th Canadian Light Aid Detachment (RCEME)
    B Squadron, 22nd Dragoons (Two Troops) - Flails
    B Coy Cameron Highlanders of Ottawa (MMG and mortars)
    14th Canadian Field Regiment - SP artillery
    19th Canadian Field Regiment - SP artillery
    52nd Canadian Anti-tank Battery (M 10 SP guns)
    247th Battery, 62nd Anti-Tank Regiment (17-pounder guns)
    80th Assault Squadron Royal Engineers - AVRE
    5th Canadian Field Company - Engineers
    16th Canadian Field Company - Engineers
    37th Canadian Light Aid Detachment (RCEME)
    C Section, 4th Canadian Provost Company
    Canadian Field Ambulance
    8th Beach Group

HQ 9th Canadian Infantry Brigade
    L Section Signals 3rd Canadian Infantry Division
    9th Canadian Infantry Brigade Defence Platoon
    The Highland Light Infantry of Canada
    The Stormont, Dundas and Glengarry Highlanders
    The North Nova Scotia Highlanders
    27th Canadian Armoured Regiment (Sherbrook Fusiliers Regiment)
    85th Canadian Light Aid Detachment (RCEME)
    C Company Cameron Highlanders of Ottawa (MMG and mortars)
    105th Anti-tank Battery, 3 Canadian Anti-tank Regiment (M10 SP guns)
    38th Canadian Light Aid Detachment (RCEME)
    D Section, 4th Canadian Provost Company
    Canadian Field Ambulance
    Detachments 103 Sub Area Beach Group

Royal Marines
    48 Commando Royal Marines
    1st Section Royal Marines Engineer Commando
    3 and 4 Batteries 2nd Royal Marines Assault Regiment
    Detachment 30 (Commando) Assault Unit Royal Marines

Divisional Troops 3rd Canadian Infantry Division
    Headquarters, 62 Anti-Tank Regiment
    32 Battery, 4th Canadian Light Anti-Aircraft Regiment
    Headquarters, Cameron Highlanders of Ottawa (mediums machine guns and mortars)

I Corps Troops
    C Squadron Inns of Court Yeomanry (Armoured cars)

21st Army Group
    79th Armoured Division
    5th Assault Regiment Royal Engineers
    Tactical Headquarters 80th Anti-Aircraft Brigade
    474th Search Light Battery (two troops)
    A Flight 652nd Air Observation Post Squadron (Ground crew)
    103 Beach Group (under command for landing)

Advice to Visitors

Preparation and planning are important prerequisites for an enjoyable and successful tour. This section aims to give some advice to those who are travelling to Normandy for the first time and acts as a checklist for the more seasoned battlefield visitor.

Travel to Normandy

Most visitors travelling to the Normandy battlefields do so by car. However, with the area's proximity to ports, an increasing number of hardy souls are cycling around the battlefields. However one chooses to travel around Normandy, a journey originating in the UK has to cross the Channel. A wide range of options available. The nearest ferry service to Juno is the Brittany Ferries route which delivers the visitor from Portsmouth to Ouistreham, less than an half an hour's drive from Juno Beach. This crossing is slightly longer than others, being six hours during the day or six hours thirty minutes overnight. Further away, just over an hour to the west, is the port of Cherbourg, which is served by sailings from Portsmouth, Southampton and Poole (three and a half hours by hydrofoil or express craft to five hours by conventional ferries). Two hours to the east is le Havre, which is served by ferries from Portsmouth and Southampton. Choice for most visitors depends on the convenience of the sailing times and, of course, relative costs. To the east of Normandy are the shorter, and consequently cheaper, crossings in the Boulogne and Calais area. For those who dislike ferries there is the Channel Tunnel, but this option, though quicker, is usually more expensive. From the Calais area, Arromanches can be easily reached via the new autoroutes in just over four hours but bear in mind tolls cost up to £15. This can be reduced to about £10 by avoiding the new *Pont de Normandie*. It is worth checking out all the options available and make your selection of routes based on UK travel, ferry times and cost. French law requires you to carry a full driving licence and a vehicle registration document. Do not forget your passport and a GB sticker if you do not have EU number plates with the blue national identifier square.

Insurance

It is important to check that you are properly insured to travel to France. Firstly, check with your insurance broker to ensure that you are covered for driving outside the UK and, secondly, make sure you have health cover. Form E111, available from post offices, grants the bearer reciprocal treatment rights in France but, even so, the visitor may wish to consider a comprehensive package of travel insurance. Such packages are available from a broker or travel agent. It is a legal requirement for a driver to carry a valid certificate of motor insurance. Be warned that without insurance, repatriating the sick or injured is very expensive, as is return of vehicles.

Accommodation

There are plenty of accommodation options in the resorts of Lagrune, St Aubin, Bernières and Courseulles. These vary from very well run campsites, through B and B accommodation to a variety of good hotels and a wide range of local restaurants. Up to date contact details are available from the French Tourist Office, 178 Picadilly, London W1V 0AL (01891 244 123). Further details of accommodation and travel amenities are available from the office of Calvados Tourisme, Place du Canada, 14000 Caen, France. To telephone from the UK dial 0033, drop the 0 necessary for ringing within France and dial 2 31 86 53 30.

While there is easily accessible information on the variety of hotel accommodation to suit all tastes and pockets, increasing numbers of visitors are using the mobile homes and the campsites in the Juno area. The main mobile park, Camping de la Cote de Nacre, which also offers camping, is located on the outskirts of St Aubin. The self-catering mobile homes can be booked through tour operators such as Canvas and French Life and their packages can cost little more, in May, early June and September than a standard cross Channel ferry fare. This excellent family site is a short walk from Nan Red and restaurants but has all the facilities, such as bar and an excellent swimming complex, which make it attractive for a family group. At the other end of the scale is the Courseulles Municipal campsite 'Canadian Scottish', which is located in the dunes immediately behind Mike Green Beach. It has basic but clean camping facilities and is easily accessible, being five minutes walk from Courseulles. Booking is somewhat haphazard, but it is always worth considering if this style of campsite suits your pocket and plans.

Maps

Good maps are an essential prerequisite to a successful battlefield visit. Best of all is a combination of contemporary and modern maps. The **Battleground** series of course, provides a variety of maps. However, a full map sheet enables the visitor or indeed those who are exploring the battlefield from the comfort of their armchair, to put the battle in a wider context. A contemporary 1:25,000 map sheet (Creully), overprinted with intelligence data, is available from the Keep Military Museum, Bridport Road, Dorchester, Dorset, DT1 1RN (01305264066) for £4.99 including postage and packing. It shows the woods and roads as they were before the intervention of modern agriculture. Overprinted are the German positions that had been located by the Resistance and air reconnaissance prior to the battle.

A number of modern map series are available in both the UK and Normandy. Most readily available in both countries are the Michelin 1:200,000 Yellow Series. Sheet 54 covers the British and US D Day build-up and break-out battle areas and is useful for getting around the Normandy battlefield and its ports. Better still are the *Institut Geographique* National (IGN) 1:100,000 *Serie Vert* (Green Series) maps. Sheet 6, *Caen-Cherbourg-Normandie*, covers most of the Normandy battle area. Normally only available in the UK at a specialist map shop they can, however, be procured as a special order through high street book shops such as Waterstones. The Series Vert maps have the advantage of showing contours and other details such as unmade roads and tracks. Sheet 6 is a good compromise if you are visiting several sites and wish to use a single map. The most detailed maps, readily available in France, are the *IGN Serie Bleue* in 1:25,000 scale. The Juno area is covered by the sheets: 1512 E *Caen*, which includes all of the Juno area covered in this book, along with Sword Beach. This map can normally be found in the tourist shops at Arromanches. However, if you are planning your tour well in advance, large retailers in the UK can order *Serie Bleue* maps, given sufficient notice.

Courtesy

Juno's coastal area is mainly a resort or residential area but inland the country is mainly open farmland and many of the villages were also a part of the battlefield. Please respect private property in both resort, open country and villages, particularly avoiding driving on unmade up farm tracks and entering non-public areas in villages. Adequate views of the scene of the action can be enjoyed from public land rights of way. In all cases, please be careful not to block roads by careless car parking. The people of Normandy extend a genuine welcome to those who come to honour the memory of the Allied liberators. To preserve this welcome please be courteous to the local people.

INDEX

Accommodation 189
Alanbrook, Field Marshal 12
Armour, German use of 36-37, 141-145
Armoured Vehicle Royal Engineer AVRE) 17-18, 20, 51, 60, 62, 63, 64, 66, 73-75, 88, 99, 107, 108-110, 114, 121, 147, 159, 170, 170-177, 181
Artillery 14, 16, 57, 112, 121-125, 168
Atlantic Wall 11, 15, 19, 22, 33-48, 77, 102, 119
Assembly Area Zulu 49
Bangalore Torpedo 69, 172
Banville 118, 121, 122, 124
BARBAROSSA, Operation 33
Basley 132, 137
Bayeux 43, 119, 181, 187
    Cemetery 187 Museum 187
British Broadcasting Corporation 173, 177, 178
Beny-sur-Mer 42, 56, 128-130, 132, 137, 167 185
Bernieres 55, 57, 62-68, 75, 106-108, 111, 114, 117, 118, 128, 129, 134, 181, 183, 187
BIGOT, Top Secret 26-27
BODYGUARD, Operation 37-40
Blackadder, Brigadier 131
Blumentritt, General der Infanterie 44
Bomber Command 6th Bomber Group 7
British and Canadian Army Formations:
    First Canadian Army 9, 11
    Second Army 77, 147, 171, 187
    I British Corps 23,24, 28, 164, 170
    I Canadian Corps 11
    II Canadian Corps 9, 11, 23
    XXX Corps 23,24
    1st Canadian Division 11
    2nd Canadian Division 11
    3rd British Division 24, 75, 145, 147, 152
    3rd Canadian Division 8,9, 15, 20, 21, 22, 23, 24, 28,43, 91, 118, 142, 144, 146, 152, 165, 167, 179
    Plans 24-27
    5th Canadian Armoured Div 11
    6th Airborne Division 141
    50th Division 91, 126, 179, 187
    51st Division 8, 118, 146, 170
    79th Armoured Div 8, 16-20, 24, 60, 62, 65, 73, 79, 86, 87, 107, 109, 146, 175, 187
    Polish Armoured Division 11
    2nd Canadian Armoured Brigade 20, 24, 26, 79, 81, 134, 137, 138,144

7th Canadian Infantry Brigade 20, 24, 26, 51, 53, 77-102, 104, 110, 118, 119, 121-128, 138, 139
8th Canadian Infantry Brigade 26, 51, 53, 58-77, 79, 104, 110 112, 118, 119, 134, 167
9th Canadian Infantry Brigade 22, 26, 110-112, 119, 128, 134, 137, 139, 167,168
153rd Infantry Brigade 118
231st Infantry Brigade 43
103 Beach Group 8, 24, 104, 114, 116, 118, 146, 151, 187
Units:
    Inns of Court Yeomanry 26
    22 Dragoons 19, 60, 62-64, 107, 174-178
    1st Canadian Hussars 17, 26, 53, 77-82, 84-90, 95-96
    Fort Garry Horse 8, 17, 26, 53, 60, 66, 115, 128, 132-137, 168, 179, 184
    1 Canadian Parachute Batt 27, 145
    1 Gordon Highlanders 118
    5 Black Watch 170, 186
    10 Commando 167
    30 Commando 171
    Cameron Highlanders of Ottawa 10, 122, 144, 185
    Canadian Scottish 10, 33, 82, 91, 101-102, 103, 121, 124, 127, 138, 139, 170, 181
    Chaudiere Regiment 10, 20, 30, 103-104, 111, 128, 131-132, 137, 167, 185
    Hackney Battalion The R Berkshire Regiment 184
    Highland Light Infantry of Canada 22, 31
    North Nova Scotia Regiment143
    North Shore Regiment 10, 20,53, 68-77, 132-137, 146,147-152, 155, 167, 168, 184, 186
    Queen's Own Rifles of Canada 10, 50, 53, 63-69, 128,131-132, 137, 146, 167, 185
    Regina Regiment 53, 82, 84-90, 116, 126. 137, 182
    Royal Winnipeg Rifles 10, 27,52, 53, 82, 90-101, 108, 121-123, 127, 138, 146, 181
    Stormont Glengarry and Dundas Highlanders 106
    247 Anti Tank Regiment RA 76
    5 Assault Squadron RE 172, 174-177
    6 Canadian Field Coy RCE 93, 98
    77 Assault Squadron RE 174
    80 Assault Squadron RE 60

Bretteville 138
Bruneval Raid 11, 165
Caen 23, 24, 43, 119, 141, 143, 181,187
CANLOAN 7
Carpiquet 26
Casablanca Conference 23
Casualties, Juno D Day 146
Centaur tank 60, 74, 158-161, 171
Channel Tunnel 189
Cherbourg 189
Churchill Tank 17, 187
Churchill, Winston 12, 17, 37, 182
Combined Operations, HQ 11-12, 16, 20, 27, 87, 112, 183
COSSAC 21, 31, 161-163
Courseulles 29, 43, 46, 55, 57, 77, 83, 84-90, 102, 110, 124, 126, 138, 181-183
    Museum 6, 182
Crab (Sherman Flail) 19, 20, 62, 87, 108, 175-177
Crear, General 13, 15, 31, 32
Creully 126, 177
Crocker, Lieutenant General 23, 24
Crocodile 19-20, 187
Cunningham, Brigadier 111
D7 Armoured Buldozer 100
Deception plans 37-40, 48, 167
Duplex Drive (DD) tanks 17, 51, 60, 64, 66, 69, 74, 77-82, 84-96, 119, 121
Dieppe 11-20, 91
Dives, River 41
Dorset 15
Douvres Radar Station 119, 135, 165-178, 186
    Cemetery 186-187
E 111, Form 189
Edwards, Commander Keneth
Eisenhower, General Dwight D 22, 31, 34, 179
ELM, Objective 26, 119, 127, 137, 138, 170
FABIUS, Exercise 22, 113
Falaise 141
Ferries, Cross Channel 189
Feuchtinger, Major General 141
Fontaine Henry 126
Forester, Brigadier 77
FORTITIUDE 38-40, 142
Fuhrer Order Fifty-one 34
Fuhrer Order Forty 33, 40
Garbo 39
German Army Formations:
    Army Group B 35
    Panzer Group West 37, 141, 143
    LXXXIV Corps 40-41, 43, 44, 141
    I SS Panzer Corps 37
    21st Panzer Division 33, 43, 120, 140-145, 160
    Panzer Lehr 141, 142

12th Hitlerjugend SS Panzer Division 141-143
352nd Infantry Division 41-43, 48, 119
716th Infantry Division 33, 40-48, 54, 83, 84, 119, 128, 145, 171
Units:
22 Panzer Regiment 141
125 Panzer Grenadier Regt 141
192 Panzer Grenadier Regt 142
439 Ost Barttalion 44
441 Ost Battalion 44, 101, 119, 121, 127
642 Ost Battalion 44, 83
726 Grenadier Regiment 43, 121, 124, 126, 127
736 Grenadier Infantry Regt 42, 55, 56, 62-63, 82, 101, 119, 128, 133, 137, 147, 157, 168
Gap M2 107-110, 181-182
Goebbels 33
Gold Beach 41, 43, 44, 119, 181
Graye-sur-Mer 24, 26, 82, 98, 122
Guingand, General de 31
H-Hour, time off 27
Hamerton, Second Lieutenant 19, 62-64, 107
Hill 112 121, 145
Hobart, Major General Percy 16-20
Home Guard 22
Insurance 189
Inverrary, Combined Operations Training Centre 14
Italy 11
Kammhuber Line 165, 167
Keller, Major general 20, 24, 26, 46, 51, 110, 112, 134, 167, 183
King, Right Honourable WLM 22
Lagrune-sur-Mer 42, 55, 145, 147-164, 184-185, 187
Leicester, Brigadier 'Jumbo' 152
Le Fresne-Camilly 126
le Havre 51, 83, 165
Lion-sur-Mer 147
Luc-sur-Mer 147, 152
M 10 Tank destroyer 76, 149, 161-163, 187
McNaughton, General 9
Maps 190
Marcks, General 142
Mike Sector 20, 26, 27, 42, 51, 57, 77-102, 107-112, 116, 118, 119, 121, 124, 181, 182
Montgomery, General 22, 23, 31, 34, 144, 179, 182
Morgan, Lieutenant General 20, 23, 38

Mountbatten, Adm Lord Louis 11
Nan Sector 26, 27, 42, 51, 53, 57, 58-77, 80, 84-88, 104-105, 107, 110-112, 115, 128, 134 147-164
National Archives 6
NEPTUNE, Operation 49, 50
Munro, Ross 11, 15, 28, 50, 64, 88, 96
Oak, Objective 26, 119, 138-139
Oliver, Commodore 49, 58
OMAHA 23, 27, 41, 43, 119
Orne, River 23, 24, 26, 142, 145
Ost Truppen 42, 44, 122, 124, 128, 137, 182
Ouisterham 24, 83, 145, 181, 189
OVERLORD, Operation 9, 23, 31, 37, 112, 141, 152, 167
Pas de Calais 34, 35, 38
Patton, General George 38
Petard - demolition gun 62, 74-75, 88, 159, 176
PIRATE, Exercise 15
Port en Bessin 23
Portsmouth, D Day Museum 179, 189
Radar 12, 165-175
    Freyer 165
    Radar Museum 186
    Wasserman 165
    Wurzburg 165, 170, 186
Ramsey, Admiral 50, 179
Reviers 121, 126, 138, 185-186
Richter, General 33, 40, 41, 145
Rommel, 33, 37, 43, 47, 48, 137, 141
Royal Air Force 28, 51, 55, 142, 165, 174
Royal Canadian Air Force 7, 55
Royal Engineers 17, 18, 170, 187
Royal Marines 47, 51, 55, 142, 165, 174
    4 SS Brigade 24, 147, 152, 155, 163, 171
    41 Commando 147, 152, 157, 160, 163, 171, 174, 186
    46 Commando 147, 171
    48 Commando 145, 146, 147, 152-164, 185, 187
    Royal Marine Assault Regiment 60, 158, 161
Royal Navy 27, 47, 57, 60, 77, 103, 112, 114
Royal Canadian Navy 7
Force J, 15, 27, 49, 51, 56, 58, 77
Ships: Algonquin, HMCS
    Belfast, HMS 56, 104, 179
    Diadem, HMS 56
    Hilary, HMS 28, 49, 50-51, 110, 134

Prince David, HMS 7, 104
Prince Henry, HMS 7
Ramillies, HMS 104
Sioux, HMCS 7, 56
X20, Mini Submarine 77-80
Rundstedt, Feldmarshall von 36, 37, 39, 44, 141, 143
Seulles, River 82-83, 90, 98, 124, 126, 134
Stacey, Colonel CP 6, 15, 32, 66, 126, 130, 137, 148
Sherman tank 16, 19, 149, 161, 163, 168, 175, 187
Shulman, Milton 37
SODAMINT, Exercise 21
Southwick House 30, 31, 49, 179
Speer, Albert 45
Stagg Gp Capt JM 26
St Aubin 42, 44, 55, 57, 62, 68-77, 102, 104, 105, 132, 133, 147-164, 184, 185
St Croix 121, 124-127
Stear, Lance Corporal Stuart 18, 20, 28, 30, 50, 104, 114-118
St Nazaire Raid 11
Symonds, Lieutenant General 10
Tailleville 77, 112, 119, 133-137, 167, 185
Tedder, Air Chief Marshal 30, 31
Todt Labour Oeganization 35, 45
Typhoon 57, 171, 174
Sword Beach 23, 43, 75, 142, 145, 146, 152
US Army
    First US Army Group (FUSAG) 38-39
    First US Army 23
    V Corps 23
    VII Corps 23
    UTAH Beach 23, 27, 41
Ver-sur-Mer Battery 142
Waterproofing of vehicles 21
Wiederstandnest
    WN 26 55, 145, 157-164
    WN 27 55, 62, 69-77, 102,111,128, 132, 147-157, 184
    WN 28 54, 55, 62-68, 78, 117, 128, 183
    WN 29 46, 55, 83, 84-88, 110,126, 182
    WN 31 46, 55, 83, 190-101, 181
    WN 32 191
Wurtzburg, Giant 126, 128
Yew, Objective 26, 66, 69, 119, 121, 131, 147